W9-AQO-920

Politics and Paradigms

ANDREW C. JANOS

Politics and Paradigms

CHANGING THEORIES OF CHANGE
IN SOCIAL SCIENCE

STANFORD UNIVERSITY PRESS, 1986

Stanford, California

Wingate College Library

Stanford University Press, Stanford, California

© 1986 by the Board of Trustees
of the Leland Stanford Junior University

Printed in the United States of America

CIP data appear at the end of the book

To Reinhard Bendix

HD 5706
5.0101

Preface

SINCE I CONSIDER MYSELF more of an empiricist than intellectual historian or "pure" theorist, a few words may be in order about the genesis of this study. Originally, the essay was planned as the introduction to a larger study designed to compare the politics of Eastern Europe in the pre-Communist and Communist periods. Such a comparison is apt to direct one's attention to both Communist studies and the so-called developmental literature, for the obvious reason that today the area is part of the Communist Bloc, and for the perhaps somewhat less obvious reason that prior to 1945 the problems of the area in question were analogous to those of the contemporary Third World. Comparisons, of course, lead to questions and call for explanations, and for such purposes classical and neo-classical constructs of political sociology and economy seemed on the whole to be inadequate. As these inadequacies revealed themselves, the essay grew in size and in time acquired a life of its own. Meanwhile, its focus moved beyond the confines of the Second and the Third Worlds to the problems of the First, in the quest for still more general questions and organizing schemes.

Throughout the major part of the writing of this book, during the winter and spring of 1984, I had the benefit of a sabbatical leave from my regular duties at the University of California in Berkeley, as well as of a grant from the American Council of Learned Societies, provided to subsidize the larger project on Eastern Europe. During the same period, I also received research assistance from the Institute of International Studies and the Center for Slavic and East European Studies at Berkeley.

Less tangibly, but no less significantly I profited from discussions with a number of colleagues. I am especially indebted to Reinhard Bendix, John Bendix, Clement Moore Henry, Norman Jacobson, Kenneth Jowitt, Chalmers Johnson, Atul Kohli, Nelson Polsby, Paul Thomas, and Aaron Wildavsky, who read the manuscript at various stages of its progress, and were generous with both their time and their advice. In many instances, this advice was followed and led, no doubt, to significant improvements in the quality of the text. In other instances, however, I followed my own counsel, the cogency of different arguments notwithstanding. For this reason alone, these colleagues should be absolved from any responsibility for opinions and conclusions that the reader will encounter.

Others to whom acknowledgments are due include my research assistants Victor Magagna and Susan Erickson, who spent a good many hours in tracking down bibliographical references. Somewhat less focused, but no less important, was the assistance and inspiration of graduate students in the Berkeley Political Science Department, especially of students enrolled in my graduate seminar in comparative politics in the fall semesters of 1982 and 1984, and among them especially Philip Brick, Jana Gold, Elizabeth Norville, and Brian Woodall, whose papers and comments were helpful in shaping some of my ideas and the ways of effectively communicating them. Lynne Gordon and Beverly Adams typed most of the manuscript in its several drafts. I received valuable assistance from Don Van Atta, who aided me in mastering the intricacies of word processing, corrected the manuscript, and participated

in its "technical" production. Finally, my thanks go to Grant
Barnes, the director of Stanford University Press, for taking
personal interest in this project, and to Ellen Smith for the capable copy editing of the volume.

A.C.J.

Contents

Politics and Paradigms

Introduction

AT THE TIME of this writing, more than twenty years have
passed since Thomas S. Kuhn first published his treatise *The
Structure of Scientific Revolutions*.[1] In this celebrated, as well as
controversial, volume, Kuhn pondered the history and practices of modern science and expressed the view that in order
to be effective, scientific inquiry must be based on "paradigms."[2] According to Kuhn, such paradigms are constructs
identifying broad relationships between two or more general
categories, together with some basic assumptions concerning
the nature of a larger universe. So defined, these paradigms
are not theories, for they do not provide explanations, only in-
structions as to where to go for explanations. Accordingly,
they allow us to organize research and, by structuring intellectual curiosity, provide an appropriate focus for scientific disciplines.[3]

Unfortunately, human powers of observation and extrapo-
lation are limited, and so is the useful life of intellectual constructs. Based on a series of observations and assumptions, a
paradigm is formulated and, because of its capacity to account
for all relevant facts, it gives rise to a discipline. But then, by
serendipity or by the serendipitous discovery of new methods
of observation, previously unknown facts may come to light,
and some of these may not be easily accommodated within the

existing paradigm. At this point, Kuhn suggests, a predictable sequence of events will follow. Bound emotionally and intellectually to the old paradigm, the scientific community is initially reluctant to abandon it. "Though they [eventually] may lose faith and then consider alternatives, they do not renounce the paradigm that has led them into crisis. They do not, that is, treat anomalies as counterinstances,"[4] but as mere variations on familiar themes. Still, as new facts multiply, there come to be too many pieces that do not fit the old framework of the puzzle, and after a while the sense of anomaly turns into disciplinary malaise. Some members of the scientific community may leave the field, or the discipline ceases to attract potentially available talent. In the end, the discipline may simply collapse and be struck from the list of true sciences, unless it is rescued by a dramatic breakthrough whereby its practitioners change not only their theories, but also some of their more cherished assumptions concerning the nature of reality. If these new assumptions permit the scientist to accommodate all pertinent facts and to formulate a new, richer body of theories, then the old paradigm will have been replaced "in part or in whole by an incompatible new one."[5]

The archetypal example of such a change from one paradigm to another has been provided to us by the history of modern physics. Starting from a "pre-paradigmatic" stage, physics acquired its first modern paradigm in the seventeenth century. The key relationships identified by this construct were among mass, distance, and motion (the first two explaining changes in the third), with the underlying assumption that space and time were mere coordinates, constants, or fixed entities. Having provided the basis for the Newtonian laws of general dynamics, this paradigm was able to elicit unprecedented consensus among the members of the scientific community and was to dominate all research and theorizing in the field for more than two centuries. This consensus, however, was shattered when scientists discovered the existence of subatomic particles, whose behavior seemed to defy conventional wisdom concerning the role of mass in determining velocity. A crisis did ensue and exacted its toll from the scientific community, until the anomaly was explained by the discovery that time and space were not constants but variables, capable of expanding and shrinking. At this point, the "conventional" paradigm of Newton was superseded by the new, counterintuitive paradigm of Einstein.

Kuhn's numerous critics may well be justified in questioning the universal relevance of this model. Still, the sequence of events he suggests and the concept of a paradigm shift seem to be eminently applicable to the experience of social sciences, and within them, to the experience of political inquiry.[6] In this instance, the sequence began with the rise of a three-tiered paradigm of political economy and sociology, which took shape within the historical context of the industrial revolution and which itself became one of the harbingers of the modern age. The key element of this paradigm is mastery over our physical environment through technological innovation and scientific discovery, which are seen to be the most critical sources of change in social attitudes and structures. In essence, this paradigm holds that when such innovations occur, there will be changes in social attitudes and in the social structure—the division of labor and the configuration of classes—which in turn will force or anticipate changes in the pattern of political authority, institutions, and behavior. If this is so, then the principal task of the social scientist is to seek out meaningful thresholds in human sophistication, whence we can proceed to explain critical aspects of social organization, including the organization of the state.

Reflecting the experience of the early industrial age in England and western Europe, this paradigm of social science was phenomenally successful in weaving the many threads of history into a single, coherent fabric, and for this reason acquired unprecedented prestige among the practitioners of the discipline. Thus while competing liberal and Marxist schools of thought continued to differ in their views of the social and economic system, they were in agreement as to the fundamental assumptions of the paradigm, directing their respective disciples to search for the causes of political change in the societies and economies "underlying" political authority. Objections by philosophical conservatives[7] caused barely a ripple, and the twin disciplines of political sociology and economy remained the cornerstones of comparative politics when this field became popular in the United States. In the interim, however, the attention of social scientists began to shift from the Occident to countries of the non-Western world, and it was in this broader empirical context that researchers encountered a series of phenomena that did not readily align with the assumptions of the accepted frame of reference. Almost at the same time, developments in the "advanced" industrial countries themselves shattered some elements of accepted sociological wisdom and contributed further to the sense of anomaly in the discipline. A prolonged intellectual crisis ensued, in the course of which repeated attempts were made to fit new facts into the Procrustean bed of old categories. But the anomalies could not be explained away, and in the end the crisis led to new paradigms, or new ways of raising questions about political reality.

The present essay sets out to trace this process of change from paradigm to paradigm, with two purposes in mind. One of them is to write an intellectual history, however sketchy, of the evolution of modern political science, with an emphasis on the more recent trials and tribulations of the discipline. The other purpose, oriented more toward the present than the past, is to take stock, to clarify, and to create order among the recent crop of competing theories. This, one may hope, would be to the benefit of the scholar interested in organizing empirical research and in comparing political phenomena in Western, non-Western, and Communist societies, within a single, unified intellectual construct.

In pursuit of these purposes, the study follows a rough chronological outline and is divided into chapters accordingly.

Chapter 1 is devoted to what may be described as the classical nineteenth-century paradigm of social science and its evolution from Adam Smith to Max Weber. Chapter 2 surveys the attempts of neo-classicism, mainly in the United States, to apply the categories of the classical paradigm to contemporary problems without adjusting the fundamental premises of the original construct. Chapter 3 traces the history of crisis and breakthrough in the discipline and examines three competing explanations for the dynamics of change in what has become known as the "modern world system." In Chapter 4 discussion shifts from structure to strategy and to alternative ways of managing international inequalities. This provides an opportunity to examine the implications of the paradigm shift for the study of Communist societies and to discuss the problems of Communist and "developing" societies in the same frame of reference. Chapter 5 then takes us from the peripheries to the "core" of the modern world economy and examines the problems of the discipline in dealing with the phenomenon of advanced, as opposed to early, industrial societies, mainly in the Occident. Finally, the Conclusions take stock of recent advances in the discipline and raise questions concerning both the utility and the limitations of structural and cultural paradigms in providing adequate bases for political theory.

ONE

Images of Change: The Classical Paradigm

Origins of a Paradigm: Images of Progress

Curiously perhaps, if questioned on the subject, most social scientists today would say that the classical paradigm of social science described in the Introduction was the work of Auguste Comte, the "father of sociology." Comte, an inveterate propagator of his own ideas and greatness, would undoubtedly agree. He did, after all, proclaim in his *Cours de philosophie positive*[1] that the diverse elements of a society are interrelated and hence change together. Moreover, in his self-celebrated "great discovery of the year 1822," he formulated his own concept of revolutions in human knowledge, arguing that scholarship must have an organizing concept before it can observe the world, and that disciplines must pass through the (pre-paradigmatic?) theological and metaphysical stages before they can reach their empirical, "positive," or scientific stage. Finally, he was the one to popularize, if not to invent, the label of "sociology" to designate what he believed would become a science of human progress and development.

This may not have been the first instance in history where the more reticent Britons have been upstaged by the Continent, merely because they failed to package, label, and advertise their discoveries in a more ostentatious manner.[2] But it is certainly one of the more egregious examples of denying academic credit where it is clearly due, for the paradigm had been formulated almost 50 years before Comte's "grand discovery" by a number of Scottish economists and moral philosophers, of whom Adam Smith (1723–90) was only one, albeit intellectually the most distinguished. Although his *Wealth of Nations*[3] is best remembered as a treatise on the invisible hand of the market mechanism, its volumes contain much more. They provide us with a full-blown economic theory of social change and political development (often misleadingly referred to as an economic theory of *history*).

Original as Smith's theory is, its leitmotif and point of departure were provided by William Robertson, one of his fellow Scotsmen, who forcefully reminded his disciples that in "every inquiry concerning the operation of men when united together in society, the first object of our attention should be their mode of subsistence. Accordingly as that varies, their laws and policy must be different."[4] The key variable of analysis is thus the sophistication of the economy, or, in Smith's term, the "dexterity" with which members of a given society apply themselves to the task of production.[5] For when this dexterity increases, there will be commensurate changes in the division of labor and in the patterns of ownership. Economic innovation and social change are thus interrelated, and it is in terms of this relationship that Smith identifies four historical stages of development, from hunting-gathering to pastoral, agricultural, and commercial forms of social organization.

Smith's theory of politics is part and parcel of this evolutionary scheme. If economics is a controlling force, politics is, in the language of modern social science, a dependent variable linked to the economy through the social structure. The linkage between the two is twofold, and yields a sophisticated, dual concept of politics. On the one hand, politics refers to the institutional structure of the state and to the performance of its regulatory, administrative, and adjudicating functions. The character of these is largely determined by the nature and complexity of the division of labor. On the other hand, politics is also the realm of power, or control over the institutions of the state. The pattern of this control is closely related to the ownership of the means of subsistence, of cattle in pastoral, of land in agricultural, of ships, factories, and money in commercial societies. True, as presented by Smith, this conceptualization of politics is not without some contradictions and ambiguities. For at times Smith describes the state as an instrument of the propertied classes; at other times he portrays it as an impartial entity that functions to check both the "hatred and envy of the poor" and the "ambition" of the rich.[6] Like so many others in that age of great social and political changes, Smith could not quite come to terms with the historical differences between oligarchies and the absolutist state.

These ambiguities notwithstanding, Smith succeeds in providing a coherent and internally consistent description of political change through history.[7] His point of departure is the hunting-gathering stage where there is virtually no division of labor, and no property other than the most primitive implements. In this stage, Smith finds no concentration of power and only the most rudimentary institutions of government. But pastoral and agricultural societies have more complex structures; they do possess a division of labor and permit, if not require, substantial concentrations of wealth and private property. The political corollary is a strong and coercive state, needed both to coordinate the process of production and to protect the property of the few from the "jealousies" of the many.

In sharp contrast we find that in commercial societies division of labor is highly complex, yet this complexity requires not more, but less, regulation. This is partly because the invisible hand of the market replaces political authority as a regulatory instrument and partly because there is what we would call today a larger degree of interdependence among the components of society. In Smith's view, the retinue of the landowner is subject to the lord's will and whim, but owners and workers in a commercial society are dependent on each other as the sellers and buyers of commodities. In addition, Smith tells us that in commercial societies the structure of power has undergone significant changes in comparison to the previous stages of historical development: not only has power passed from landowners to entrepreneurs, but also from the few to the many, as a result of a more equal distribution of private property. Accordingly, technological innovation and economic growth may be seen as the sources of "progress" from the "rude" to the "civilized" stages of development. For in the long run, diminishing scarcities and growing social complexities are accompanied by diminishing coercion and increasing social peace. Still, Smith's concept of progress is vastly different from that of Antoine Condorcet (1743–94) and other political romantics of his age, because it does not contemplate perfection, only steady improvement, in the condition of humanity. Thus even in the most highly developed commercial societies, Smith expected to find want, envy, conflict, and hence a need for firm political authority, if only to ensure the smooth functioning of the market mechanism.

While in and of itself this theory shows sweeping intellectual qualities, what makes it still more impressive is the way in which it is anchored in a universal theory of motivation and behavior. In this theory the pursuit of gain occupies a central position; for Smith, people are interested above all else in reducing their own dependence on nature and in increasing their share of scarce material resources and amenities. Such interests "serve to rouse and keep in continual motion the industry of mankind,"[8] that is, they explain increases in technological sophistication and the gradual improvement in material conditions that together constitute a key element of progress.

But if the pursuit of gain is the most universal of human motivations, it is not the only motivation relevant to our social existence. Next to self-love and concern for utility, Smith discerns yet another key "propensity," the desire to be approved of by others. Independently of self-interest, this desire impels persons to show "fellow feeling," or moral restraint towards others in the pursuit of gain.[9] Such fellow feeling has been "implanted in humanity by the Author of Nature,"[10] or else reflects a higher interest in the salvation of one's immortal soul that should take precedence over the pursuit of material gain. Unfortunately for humanity, although this quality is essential for maintaining stable and effective social relationships, it is not universal, as is the motivation for gain. All may need it to make progress, but only some will have it, a circumstance that—combined with a number of other conditions, such as the absence of natural resources in a region or the lack of "self-command" in its inhabitants—may well explain why not all societies of the world will be able to traverse the road from the "rude" to the "civilized" stages of social organization.[11] While many are called, few will be chosen. Quite clearly, Smith borrowed the theme from Protestant moral philosophy. But in time, stripped of its theological trappings, the idea would reappear in sociology and political science to form the nucleus of various theories of political culture and of cultural theories of development.[12]

The far better known, and in our own days perhaps more influential, Marxist theory of development owes a great deal to Smith and shares a number of common elements. Like Smith, Marx (1818–83) takes the process of production as the point of departure for his theory. He believes that this process, or the "mode" of production, determines the "relationships of production," that is, the way in which the division of labor, property ownership, and modes of exchange are institutionalized. He then goes on to designate changes in the technology of production as the "demiurge" of change in history.[13] Much like Smith, Marx also defines thresholds in the process of technological change in order to formulate his own historical stages of development, from primitive communism to slavery, feudalism, and capitalism. The choice of these stages, particularly the third and fourth, reflects Marx's Central European education with its emphasis on the history of the Middle Ages and antiquity (as opposed to Smith's broader British familiarity with exotic societies on different continents). Nonetheless, the initial Marxian model of the *Communist Manifesto, German Ideology,* and the *Grundrisse,* becomes more closely aligned with Smithian thinking in the first volume of *Capital,* in which Marx examines the rise of modern Europe and distinguishes between agricultural, commercial, and industrial phases in the development of capitalism.[14]

Within this overall scheme, Marx is also heavily influenced by Smith's political sociology. As with Smith, politics is a dependent variable: in Marx's well-known terminology it is part of the "superstructure" that rests on an economic base. Thus when the latter changes, the former will collapse and will have to be rebuilt. Again, as in the thinking of Smith, the political realm has several components: it encompasses the state as an institution, power as the function of ownership, and consciousness shaped by economic realities. The effects of economic change on politics are thus threefold: first, technological innovation creates new complexities as well as an incongruity between old institutions and the new division of labor; second, technological innovation creates new forms of ownership and hence a new class of potential rulers; third, changes in technology create new forms of political consciousness, thus undermining the validity of ideas used to justify the old system of rule.[15] Of these three relationships, Marx was most interested in the nexus between economic and political power, perhaps least interested in the institutions of the state, which he tended to dismiss as mere instruments of the dominant economic class. On this last point Marx was more forceful than Smith, though over the years a few notes of doubt crept into his thinking as he pondered the possible autonomy of the state from economic classes in his studies of oriental despotism and the Bonapartist state of his own days.[16]

Next to these similarities, however, we must also recognize

significant differences between Smithian and Marxian thinking. Indeed, these differences provide us with a catalogue of contrasts between liberal and radical concepts of development that are just as pertinent today as they were a hundred years ago. The first of these differences stems from Marx's Ricardian view of the market as a fundamentally flawed and imperfect allocative mechanism. Though on the whole Marx agrees that commodities are exchanged at a rate reflecting reciprocal utilities, he sees one major exception to the rule—the most important, the "ultimate" commodity, labor, is exchanged for less than its utility to the entrepreneur. "The worker receives means of subsistence in exchange for his labor power, but the capitalist receives in exchange for his means of subsistence labor, the productive activity of the worker, the creative power whereby the worker not only replaces what he consumes but *gives to the accumulated labor a greater value than it previously possessed.*"[17] (Italics in original.) As to why this should be so, why the laborer should sell his labor power below its value in use, Marx is somewhat ambivalent. At times he suggests that this is a matter of coercion pure and simple, exercised ultimately through the institutions of the state. On other occasions, however, he seems to suggest that this is the result of a virtually unlimited supply of labor, of a perennial buyer's market, in which competition forces laborers to exchange their labor power at the cost of mere physical subsistence. Either way, the expropriation of laborers becomes an integral part of relationships of production in all class societies, but especially under capitalism, where the expropriated surplus exceeds the consumer needs of the ruling class and, through accumulation, turns into capital—accumulated, or indirect, labor—for the creation of further surplus.

This theory of surplus value, then, is at the heart of Marx's general analysis of capitalism and, more specifically, of his theory of immiseration, first expounded in "Wage Labour and Capital" and elaborated fully in his *Capital*. We have seen above how labor exchanged for the means of subsistence can turn itself into capital and into profit for the capitalist. However, because of the internal contradictions of the system, the capitalist cannot quietly enjoy these fruits of exploitation; the market will pit producer against producer, forcing them to sell their commodities ever cheaper in a struggle for economic survival. And in order "to be able to sell more cheaply without ruining himself, he must produce more cheaply . . . by a greater division of labor, by more universal introduction and continual improvement of machinery."[18] But these changes in the "organic composition of capital" (the ratio between "direct labor" and "indirect labor," that is, labor capitalized in the form of machinery) will have debilitating consequences for the mass of laborers. They will enable one worker to do the work of many, thus intensifying competition among the workers themselves and depressing further the average wage. Moreover, as work is simplified in this manner, "the special skill of the worker becomes worthless."[19] Ironically, Marx concludes "as labor becomes more unsatisfying, more repulsive, competition increases and wages decrease."[20] In the short run, this condition may be tenable. But in the long run, the downward spiral of immiseration will produce massive social dissatisfaction that will intensify the struggle between classes and ultimately bring down the edifice of capitalism.

True, in developing this theory, Marx would note exceptions to the rule and could conceive of situations in which productive capital would grow rapidly enough to generate sufficient demand for labor and so drive wages upward rather than downward. But even if wages consistently increased, capitalism would still be doomed, for

the rapid growth of productive capital [would] bring about an equally rapid growth of wealth, luxury, social wants, and social enjoyments. Thus, although the enjoyments of the worker have risen, the social satisfaction that they give has fallen in comparison with the increased enjoyments of the capitalist, which are inaccessible to the worker, in comparison with the state of development of society in general. Our desires and pleasures spring from society; we measure them, therefore, by society and not by the objects which serve for their satisfaction. Because they are of a social nature, they are of a relative nature.[21]

Perhaps unbeknownst to him, Marx created here a theory of relative deprivation that has less to do with exploitation than with the basics of human nature, for the sense of deprivation apparently will increase whether the condition of inequality is the result of exploitation or not. This is still more evident from the following rarely quoted passage on the subject of immiseration and revolution:

A house may be large or small; as long as the surrounding houses are equally small it satisfies all social demands for a dwelling. But let a palace arise beside the little house, and it shrinks from a little house to a hut. The little house shows now that its owner has only very slight or no demands to make; and however high it may shoot up in the course of civilisation, if the neighboring palace grows to an equal or even greater extent, the occupant of the relatively small house will feel more and more uncomfortable, dissatisfied and cramped within its four walls.[22]

A further contrast with Smith arises from Marx's theory of motivation. This theory, like Smith's, rests on the concepts of gain and self-interest. But unlike Smith, who distinguishes between economic and social propensities—or, in our contemporary terminology, between class interest and culture—Marx puts the weight of explanation on the former and denies the independence of the latter. It is not that Marx is oblivious to the existence of "fellow feeling" among humans or of the virtues of "self-command" and restraint, including the ability of a ruling class to put honor ahead of monetary gain. Indeed, he realizes that feudal aristocracies may adhere to codes of honor that make them shun pecuniary reward. However, such codes could be explained, not by commitments to "higher" ideals, but by enlightened self-interest and the rational calculation of long-term gain. If aristocrats abide by codes of honor, this is mainly because such codes are expressions of a class solidarity that permits the effective exercise of class power and the reaping of long-run collective benefit. What appears to be an independent variable in the classical liberal scheme is for Marx a category that can be readily extrapolated from the prevailing division of labor and configurations of class interests. Culture thus becomes a dependent or, more accurately, epiphenomenal variable that can be reduced in toto to the socio-economic structure. Borrowed by Marx from Bentham, this is an interest theory of motivation par excellence.

Finally, and perhaps most significantly, differences between the two schemes arise from the Hegelian dialectic that infuses every aspect of Marxist thinking about society and history. Often described as a "method," this dialectic may just as well be characterized as a universal theory of action that sees humans struggling to cope with problems created by their environment. As these problems, or challenges, arise humans will design solutions, only to find that the solutions have produced new problems. The reason for this is, to use the terminology of modern theories of organization, the bounded rationality of the actors—that is, their inability to grasp the significance of all variables affecting potential outcomes. This mode of thinking, of course, did not originate with Hegel, but with the Greek philosophers of antiquity, for whom it suggested a cyclical model of being that embraced both development and decay. What Hegel added to dialectic was a large dose of optimism, a belief that with every new confrontation and collapse, humanity moves one step closer to comprehensive rationality and hence to perfection in design. Thus cycle becomes progress, while progress itself acquires a millenarian cast that Marx shared with other revolutionary optimists.

In a sense, therefore, Marx is a synthesizer, and his most formidable accomplishment is his synthesis of these Hegelian notions of change and Smith's economic theory of history. He achieves this by identifying the fundamental human "problem" as one of acquisition, of overcoming scarcity. The periodic revolutions in the means of production are, in effect, attempts to find solutions to this overriding problem. These, however, are bound to fail, given the fundamental imperfections of all historically known forms of social and institutional order. Thus while human ingenuity is capable of inventing new technologies to multiply the fruits of labor, these inventions cannot solve the problem of scarcity as long as they are put to work in the institutional context of private ownership, which breeds new forms of inequality every day. Indeed, one of the major contradictions of history is that the greater the productive potential of society, the greater the accompanying inequality. Capitalism, while representing a "higher" stage of development, is more exploitive than feudalism.

Nonetheless, capitalism, especially its industrial stage, will accomplish a dual task: first, it will create modern technology and hence objective conditions for the satisfaction of basic human needs; second, by combining its sophistication with savage exploitation, it will erase the false consciousness of the masses that has permitted their exploitation throughout history. The masses, in other words, will reach a state of comprehensive rationality. Once this happens, the world will be ready for the resolution of fundamental historical contradictions by abolishing private property, for the creation of a society of plenty, equality, and harmony in a fifth and terminal stage of history that Marx, under the label of socialism, adds to the four-stage developmental scheme of classical liberalism.

The Politics of Differentiation: From Spencer to Durkheim

The theories of both Smith and Marx were primarily inspired by the British historical experience. In this experience, highly personalized feudal relationships among lords and retainers were gradually replaced by exchange relationships of a more impersonal nature, and the rise of markets was accompanied by economic growth, that is, by spurtlike increases in the potentially available pool of social goods. From observations of the market and diminishing scarcities, Smith and Marx derived their concepts of developmental stages and, by extending them backward—or, in the case of Marx, backward and forward—in time, their economic theories of change. The experience of industrialism is woven into both theories, but it is not the key or defining characteristic of the modern age. Neither Marx nor Smith, it should be remembered, wrote about "industrial societies," but about exchange, and they chose to describe their images of contemporary society under the labels of commercialism and capitalism respectively.

In contrast to this emphasis on exchange, many contemporary and later thinkers focused their attention on the causes and consequences of industrialism. Some of these theories are highly optimistic, reflecting the early success of the industrial revolution of England. Others are ambivalent or downright pessimistic about the liberal state—and, more generally, about the human condition—in the modern age. In either case, we deal here with a new type of political theory, the pivotal concern of which is not with the distribution of scarce resources, but with growing social differentiation and complexity. The critical relationship here is between society and the machine. As the means of production become more and more sophisticated, there will be an increasing number of social roles performed by fewer and fewer persons. Differentiation thus implies both growing social complexity and functional specialization, and it is in terms of these two interrelated variables that we can make comparisons among societies at different levels of development.

The most important of these theorists of industrial society, and the single most influential liberal sociologist of the nineteenth century, was Herbert Spencer (1822–1903), author of the monumental *Principles of Sociology*.[23] A writer most popular with the educated classes of Britain, Spencer (like many of his later American counterparts after World War II) was a developmental consultant to a number of governments.[24] Much like the work of his great predecessors, Spencer's contributions to social science were the product of prior revolutions in natural science. But where Marx and Smith had been rather un-self-conscious beneficiaries of the equilibrium models of Newton-

ian physics, Spencer was a conscious imitator of the Lamarckian and Darwinian revolutions, introducing biological and
organic analogies into political sociology.[25] And where the
Smithian and Marxian "systems," or equilibrium models of society, encompassed theories of individual motivation and behavior—permitting their authors to approach reality at two
different levels of analysis and to explain the behavior of the
whole in terms of the behavior of its parts—Spencer's theory
is starkly holistic. In it society is an "organic aggregate,"[26] the
existence of which supersedes the existence of its parts. Indeed, the parts acquire existence and meaning only in the context of the whole, which therefore should be treated as a living
organism in its physical environment.[27]

Spencer's justification for the organic analogy is multifold.[28]
First, like the limbs, the brain, and the stomach, the parts of
society are interdependent. "Injury to one hurts [all] others."[29]
Second, these parts all perform functions to keep the larger
entity alive—analogous to the nutritive, locomotive, regener-
ative, and procreative functions in the living organism—and
no part can function without the others. As in the case of living organisms, the number of these functions is limited and a
priori discernible; hence it is in terms of these that we can
most profitably compare and classify societies. Politics in this
analogy is like the brain or nervous system,[30] the functions of
which are to command, to regulate, and to coordinate the
functioning of the other elements of the system. Third, societies, like living organisms, are driven by their inner nature to
adapt themselves to their environment, and successful adaptation implies differentiation in the structure of the entity. As
in the Lamarckian system, differentiation means not only
change but progress, for increasing complexity and specialization of functions are assumed to produce a greater capacity
to respond to the challenges of the environment. More differentiated societies in the Spencerian system will be more adept
at solving their problems and at surviving in a world of competing nation states.

Spencer has an additional reason to equate differentiation with progress, and this equating represents the centerpiece of his political sociology. As societies rise on the evolutionary ladder from simple to compound, and then to "doubly and trebly compound," stages of development, or from agrarian to industrial organization, they leave behind the malignant passions and the "savage improvidence" of earlier, more primitive stages of social existence.[31] This is not only because of increasing abundance, as we have seen in the Smithian scheme, but also because of increasing interdependence among the individual parts, which will virtually mandate cooperative behavior. The logic of Spencer's organic analogy is the logic of social peace and political pluralism. In a complex society, cooperation is a must; without it society cannot function and exist. And since differentiation is an open-ended process, there is virtually no limit to progress and the degree of civility and cooperation that human societies can achieve.

Through these premises and syllogisms, Spencer produced his own brand of social utopianism, his own version of the withering away of the state. Still, there is one important difference between the optimism of Marx and that of Spencer, which, more than any other, sets apart liberal from Marxist thinking about evolutionism. For while Marx and other philosophical radicals believed that progress was to be universal, Spencer, in the fashion of Smith, taught that only some societies were qualified to reach the higher stages of development. True, in Spencer, Smith's theological-cultural concept of virtue was replaced by the Darwinian theory of random selection and the survival of the fittest.[32] But in either case, the number of these lucky societies was to be very few. In Spencer's own time, the club of "true" industrial societies was an exclusive one: it included, of course, Britain; otherwise Spencer recognized as industrial only the Low Countries, the Hanse, and the United States.[33] Most of the societies of the world, among them the colonies of Britain, were hunting-plundering societies. A few others, like Germany and Russia, were seen to have an industrial "sector." But this sector existed only as a "permanent commissariat . . . solely to supply the needs of the governmental-military structures."[34] Thus, like the subject peoples, the great power rivals of England were described as societies at lower rungs of the evolutionary ladder, naturally inferior to Britain, the most highly developed society of the world. Whatever Spencer's intent, his "objective social science" became a powerful intellectual instrument to justify the primacy of Britain in the international order.

The first of the great continentals to develop a sociological theory of history was Auguste Comte (1798–1857), who may now enter our pantheon of classical nineteenth-century social science. The span of his life and work overlaps with Marx and Spencer, though not, as we noted earlier, Adam Smith. As an assistant to Saint-Simon, he inherited the interest of the latter in industrialism and developed it further into a full-fledged theory of change. In brief, Comte's theory, which he liked to refer to as the "great discovery of the year 1822,"[35] hinges on the concept of expanding knowledge, or, in Comte's own words, on the "growth of the human mind,"[36] defined as the capacity to understand and master the physical environment. Given this definition, Comte saw as his main task the identification of appropriate thresholds, which he accomplished by distinguishing among theological, metaphysical, and scientific stages. In each stage, institutions and social arrangements reflect these particular forms of consciousness. Like Spencer after him, Comte speaks of military and industrial societies (corresponding to the theological and scientific stages), with the intermediate, metaphysical stage identified with the legal state—the fundamental difference among them being the "distribution of different human occupations . . . and the growing complexity of the social mechanism."[37]

Like Spencer, Comte also believes in the gradual progression of civility, expressed by the transfer of loyalties from the tribe to the nation, and from the nation to humanity. But unlike Spencer, Comte views society, not as an organic entity, but as an entity held together by beliefs, and these beliefs, Comte fears, might be undermined by differentiation and growing complexity. The same principle that makes society advance also threatens to "decompose" it.[38] The future is therefore uncertain. On the one hand, scientific consciousness holds out the prospect of a universal state. On the other, there is a chance that this state might turn out to be harsh and oppressive, for only a strong state can "contain and so far as possible arrest" the centrifugal forces inherent in complex social organization, and "sustain continuously the idea of the whole and the sentiment of common solidarity" by intervening "appropriately in the daily performance of all the various functions of the social economy."[39] Though Spencer and Comte were looking at the same reality, their different modes of thinking led them to different predictions about the future of the modern world.

If Comte was ambivalent, some of his German colleagues were downright gloomy about the prospects for humanity. One of them was Ferdinand Tönnies (1855–1936), who, like Spencer, described social change as passage between two now famous ideal types, between *Gemeinschaft* and *Gesellschaft*. The difference between the two is in terms of scale, complexity, and the division of labor. The concept of market exchange also creeps into the overall picture, so that the features of industrialism and commercialism—functional specialization and the loss of affect—merge into a single, forbidding model. Thus in a *Gesellschaft* we will

find not action that can be derived from an *a priori* and necessarily existing unity. . . . On the contrary, here everybody is by himself and isolated, and there exists a condition of tension against all others. Nobody wants to grant and produce for another individual, if it be not in exchange for a gift of labor equivalent to what he considers at least equal to what he has given.[40]

Complexity and selfishness here go together and invite a strong state "to keep within bounds all those particular wills, all those individual interests."[41] This is a far cry, not only from

Spencer's exuberant optimism, but also from Comte's qualified optimism and ambivalence.

Just as pessimistic as Tönnies is another great continental, Emile Durkheim (1858–1917), who, like Spencer and Smith before him, focuses our attention on the division of labor. He sees change as adaptation to contingencies by technical innovation, which he then relates to the differentiation of the social structure. Like Spencer's social system, Durkheim's progresses from lower to higher stages by acquiring greater complexity. But again, the process is fraught with peril for humanity. "According to the economists," Durkheim tells us, "the division of labor is caused by the need for increasing happiness. This supposes that we really are becoming happier. Nothing is less certain."[42]

This pessimism is closely related to Durkheim's concept of the social system. While at times Durkheim appears to be attracted to the notion of interdependence and flirts with the idea of a self-sustaining social system,[43] in its mature form, the "integration" of the Durkheimian system derives from culture—that is, from a system of symbols that links individuals to society by providing them with a sense of identity and with a set of norms appropriate to the division of labor. Social change, then, is not only a matter of differentiation, but also of transformation in the systems of solidarity and integration. The most sweeping of these changes in history is the change from mechanical solidarity based on ritual to solidarity based on deliberately designed cults, myths, and social doctrines.

Durkheim's pessimism stems from his view that as society experiences greater degrees of differentiation, the norms guiding the individual may lag behind the rate of social change. Marx, of course, had to face this fact too, but he preferred to treat it as an exception, something that happens only occasionally. For Durkheim, such a lag in consciousness is more a rule than an exception. It is a concomitant of social change, responsible for anomie, or normlessness, a state of affairs that implies personal disorientation and social strain. Although a new culture may arise to fill the void and to provide standards of conduct appropriate to the new situation, the "re-integration" of society is by no means certain. In the absence of social norms, the personality may simply collapse. In the most extreme case, individuals may resolve the crisis by committing suicide. Or they may seek relief at the expense of society, by joining radical sects, whose very identity derives from negating the larger social system. What then provides the source of normality to the individual becomes a source of morbidity for society at large.

Durkheim's pessimism is particularly profound when it comes to modern society, for two reasons. First, Durkheim suggests, in modern society the rate of change will be particularly great, and the disjuncture between social structure and norms may become endemic rather than transitional. Second, Durkheim appears to be diffident about the effectiveness of modern secular belief systems and their ability to "have the same effect as the multitude of extinguished beliefs."[44] In the modern world, Durkheim writes, the "individual [himself] becomes the object of a sort of religion."[45] While this secular cult "turns all will toward the same end, this end is not social. . . . It is still from society that it takes all its force, but it is not to society that it attaches us; it is to ourselves."[46] Hence, the ideology of individualism and of personal dignity may not provide a true social link. As in the theories of Comte and Tönnies, in Durkheim's too the void will likely be filled by a strong state, itself free from moral considerations and restraints. Together with a "strain theory" of human motivation, there arise here the dark contours of a future theory of totalitarian modernity.

Max Weber: The Politics of Routinization and Rationality

Although Durkheim has given us the concept of integration, he has not developed it into a full-fledged theory. He does, in other words, tell us that differentiation raises the prospects of cultural crisis and psychological strain. But he does not tell us, in a clear-cut manner, when and how integration will be attained, or whether new beliefs arise by deliberate endeavor or in response to the needs of the social system. No one seems to be more aware of this than Claude Lévi-Strauss. In his words, Durkheim realizes that "all social life . . . presupposes intellectual activity of which the formal properties . . . cannot be a reflection of the concrete organization of society,"[47] but he shrinks back from drawing the obvious conclusion from this proposition, and in the end "make[s] symbolism grow out of society."[48]

One of the great accomplishments of Max Weber (1864–1920) is that he clearly understands this dilemma and attempts to provide a solution by bringing together two seemingly conflicting strands of nineteenth-century social thought. On the one hand, Weber, like Marx, suggests that human action is best understood as a reflection of self-interest, a category that has its roots in social class and status. On the other hand, he is also keenly aware that action cannot be divorced from "systems of meaning" (*Sinnzusammenhänge*), which, as "definitions of situations,"[49] impinge on the ways in which actors pursue their self-interest. So defined, these systems of meaning become key elements of culture. When they collapse under the cumulative weight of structural change, society and the individual will experience strain, not unlike the strain produced by Durkheim's anomie.

At this point, however, Durkheim and Weber seem to part company. Whereas Durkheim sees change essentially as a one-way street from equilibrium to disequilibrium and strain, Weber, inspired by Georg Simmel (1858–1918), can easily conceive of development as a two-way street, going from equilibrium to strain, and then from strain back to equilibrium again. Out of chaos order may arise either by a process of retraditionalization (*Vergemeinschaftung*) or by the establishing of a new social contract (*Vergesellschaftung*). The key to the outcome is Weber's charismatic leader, to whom people will turn in mo-

ments of anxiety and distress. True, charisma is one of Weber's least well-defined concepts: the charismatic leader is a
man (or woman) for all seasons. Most of the time, he is described as a figure who, by the sheer force of personal mag-
netism, can negate all established rules and structures and
hence is instrumental in prolonging chaos and fluidity in society. But he may also be a hero who, by the force of personal
example, can validate systems of norms, or he may be a
"prophet," a person who "reveals and ordains . . . normative
patterns,"[50] who can provide "a unified view of the world derived from a consciously integrated and meaningful attitude
toward life. To the prophet, both the life of man and the
world, both social and cosmic events, have a systematic and coherent meaning. To this meaning the conduct of mankind
must be oriented if it is to bring salvation."[51]

The prophet is, then, a creator of culture. By introducing
him, Weber, more than any other sociologist of the age, takes
us to the crossroads of history and social science, to the point
in history where the role of social forces ends, and that of the
individual begins.

However, Weber's theory deals with changes not only in the
degree but also in the kind of beliefs that inform human attitudes and behavior. These changes are summarized in his theory of rationalization, a process defined by him as the devaluation of tradition in human affairs.[52] In reality, the term
relates not to one but to three analytically separate, though interrelated, processes, corresponding to Weber's three separate
definitions of tradition. The first of these concepts derives
from the juxtaposition of habit with deliberate choice and the
progressive "systematization of conduct," or the calculation of
cost and benefit, as in the case of rational accounting.[53] In the
second instance, Weber contrasts the traditionalism of the kinship group with the rationality of the market, a place that people enter, not to commune with friends or kinsmen, but to sell
their commodities to the highest bidder. In this sense, ratio-

nalization means the progressive devaluation of kinship and the progressive commercialization of social relations.[54]

Finally, rationalization derives from a juxtaposition of the sacred with the secular and utilitarian, and refers to the gradual demystification (*Entzauberung*) of the world in the wake of scientific and technological progress. This third aspect of rationalization is the linchpin of the theory and transforms it from a purely descriptive into an explanatory construct. It also grounds it, in the Comtian and Marxian fashion, in control over the material environment. Pre-modern people observed the phenomenon of lightning and suffered from plagues, without being able to understand either. Not being able to account for them rationally, they fell back on transcendental explanations and attempted to protect themselves by resorting to magic, ritual, and taboo.[55] In contrast, modern people understand electricity and microorganisms, and use lightning rods and medicine to forestall the ill effects of natural events. Progress from one condition to another has had a profound impact on the human mind: although the idea of the transcendental has not disappeared, it has become devalued and increasingly remote from everyday concerns. "Modern man," writes Weber, "even with the best of will is unable to give religious ideas the same significance for culture and national character, which they deserve."[56] Thus in the Occident, at least, the religious roots of society have been disappearing slowly, giving way to "utilitarian worldliness."[57] In the last analysis, it is this very worldliness—and the remoteness of transcendental sanction—that permits individuals to abandon their next of kin or to abandon the immortal precepts of ancestors, to seek instead profit in the economic market.

Weber's theory of political change arises out of this general theory. In the center of the theory are living ideas, or beliefs; when some of these beliefs change, with them will change all aspects of social life: politics, economics, the arts, music, and even religion will move from traditional to rational patterns.

In politics, change will be manifest at three separate levels, again reflecting Weber's threefold understanding of traditionalism and rationality. First, the rationalization of politics means the demystification of authority, the devaluation of divine right, and its replacement with secular utility: from an instrument of divine will, the state will turn into an instrument of society and of its interests. At the second level, the rationalization of authority refers to the systematization of political conduct: the rise of modern bureaucracies and the professionalization of politics. Finally, the rationalization of politics means the adaptation of the market principle to political authority, by creating a political arena in which public office is "auctioned off" to the highest bidder.

This last aspect of the theory, of course, refers to the democratization of politics, which liberal political scientists of recent decades have occasionally made into the centerpiece of their own thinking. Weber himself was more pessimistic about politics in the modern world. For one thing, he anticipated that conflicts would arise between democracy and bureaucracy, in which the victory of the former was by no means assured. But even if democracy were victorious, it could easily be rendered meaningless by the demystified worldliness of the modern age, which might well turn society into an "iron cage," a cold, impersonal place populated by "nullities," who delude themselves that they have "attained a level of civilization never before achieved."[58] There is only one ray of hope in the unremitting darkness of this picture—the prospect of the "rebirth of old ideas and ideals," through the medium of prophetic revelation and leadership.[59] These observations on the closing pages of *The Protestant Ethic and the Spirit of Capitalism* do not turn Weber into a theorist of cycles, but together with the concepts of *Vergemeinschaftung* and *Vergesellschaftung*, make him a more flexible evolutionist thinker than most of his contemporaries.

The synthesizing intent is equally evident in Weber's concept of power, which, like his theory of change, is woven together from two conflicting intellectual strands. On the one hand, Weber views politics from the "top down," that is, from the perspective of the "chief" and his "administrative staff." This puts him in the same class with Marx (as well as with conservatives like Pareto and Mosca) and sets him apart from Bentham, Mill, de Tocqueville, Bentley, Bryce, and a host of other students of Anglo-Saxon politics. Whereas the concern of the latter group is with the ways in which an enlightened public can impose its will upon its government, Weber's principal concern is with the ways in which governments can elicit compliance and obedience from their subjects. Still, Weber's view of hierarchy is not one of strict asymmetry. Unlike Marx's ruling class (and Pareto's elite), Weber's chief and his administrative staff can elicit compliance only in exchange of some gift, be it a miracle or daily bread. This is, in other words, a system of reciprocity, in which the chiefs can rule effectively only if they satisfy some expectation on the part of their subordinates. True, there are instances when, as Weber notes, chiefs can rule by force alone and can "afford to drop even the pretense of a claim for legitimacy."[60] But if they do so, they must still cater to the needs of their retinue and auxiliaries. At one level or another, then, the system requires consent. Authority implies the consent of some to the exercise of force over others.

Underlying this concept of hierarchy is Weber's fundamentally rationalistic view that individuals are capable of discerning their needs and of acting upon them in a consistent way. In this rationalistic framework, need is socially determined and is independent from the volition of rulers. Thus although in the Weberian concept legitimacy may not rest on truth as it exists "out there," it is not pure fraud or false consciousness either, but a matter of belief that, beyond certain limits, is not subject to clever manipulation. Elites in this system have to "represent," if not formal constituencies, then at least the cultural expectations of their subjects.

This, then, takes us to the Weberian concept of system,

which becomes intelligible only if we draw a sharp distinction between ideas and beliefs. As pure abstractions, ideas belong in the realm of philosophy, while belief is the raw material for sociology and political science. Weber, of course, was a social scientist. Still, in order to construct his *Herrschaftssystem*, he turns to the purely symbolic. His system of authority, or political order, has nothing to do with equilibrium or interdependence, as does the system of Spencer; it acquires systemic qualities in that the relationship expresses certain ultimate principles and hence exists only as a logical relationship. It is in this sense that the Weberian system (of charismatic, rational-legal, and traditional authority) is an ideal type, which turns into reality only if principle, or idea, turns into belief for a substantial number of actors. If this is indeed the case, then, by sheer logic we can predict the nature of the political order: the logic of charismatic salvationism, for instance, will predict the fluidity of political reality and the absence of formal, institutional restraints. But in real life, these principles will rarely be shared by all important actors, and the less the degree of consensus, the less the congruence between ideal type and reality. This being the case, the Weberian ideal type is less useful in predicting reality than in directing our attention to discrepancies between logic and reality, and hence to the sources of tension and instability in the political system.

TWO

Neo-Classicism: Variations on a Theme

Early Revisionism: Veblen and Lenin

Individually and collectively, these bodies of thought—of Smith, Marx, Spencer, Durkheim, and Weber—have had an enormous intellectual impact on social thinking, and rightly so. They identified a number of critical elements in the social process and reduced the infinitely complex historical experience of the Occident to a few manageable categories. If nothing else, they left behind a number of convenient shorthands that no student of the Western world could henceforth ignore, and this achievement has won popularity for these theories among both historians and social scientists. However, the same achievement has also raised vexing questions concerning their universal validity. For once the theories were taken outside the narrow confines of the Occident, they could not fully account for the social and political patterns encountered.

One of the earliest attempts at revising classical theories of unilinear development was made by the American economist Thorstein Veblen (1857–1929), as he compared the histories of England and Germany in the industrial age. From his comparisons Veblen quickly concluded that Germany was not about to replicate the British experience, but rather was on its way to create a new form of industrial civilization. Above all,

Veblen observed the great economic success of imperial Germany and attributed it to a "situational advantage" that late industrializers enjoy over the early ones.[1] According to Veblen there were three sources of this advantage. First, "a new technology comes into the hands of [the borrower] in the shape of a theoretical principle rather than in the shape of a concrete expedient within the limits of traditional use."[2] The backward country will borrow technologies without a broad range of wasteful "usages, conventions, vested rights, canons of equity and propriety."[3] Second, because it is introduced from the outside, borrowed rather than invented, technology will have the effect of disrupting old habits and customs that would impede the rational functioning of the modern industrial economy. Third, backward countries, Veblen suggests, might escape the phenomenon of "depreciation by obsolescence,"[4] for they will always be able to introduce the most advanced technology available at a given historical moment and thus avoid having to pay the price of experimentation. One example cited by Veblen is the railroad. Whereas the British, who had invented it, "got stuck with their narrow tracks and silly little bobtailed carriages,"[5] their German imitators based their entire system on newly developed broad-gauged tracks. The British, Veblen observed with considerable detachment, "have not sinned against the canons of technology. It is only that they pay a penalty for having been thrown into the lead."[6]

Veblen's bold theory came down on the side of the latecomer mainly because he failed to understand that alongside potential advantages, backward countries also faced serious disadvantages, especially with respect to capital formation. Nor did he appreciate the adverse political consequences of cultural strain created by the borrowing of alien technologies and institutional arrangements. Yet Veblen did not predict the free and easy passage of all backward societies to the stage of advanced industrialism. Rather, he saw economic success as the function of configurations in what we today would call political culture as shaped by the vagaries of national historical experience. Thus while many countries of his time may have possessed the situational advantages of backwardness, not all possessed the "predatory cultural pedigree of Prussia"[7] that permitted Germany to turn potential into reality. Specifically, it was this cultural pedigree, with its "medieval militarism" and "authentic sense of fealty,"[8] that encouraged the rise of an all-powerful state whose institutions Veblen regarded as economically more efficient than the "anarchic" individualism of the Anglo-Saxon countries. The future thus belonged not to all latecomers, but to latecomers with a strong statist-collectivist tradition, like Germany, Japan, and Russia, which Veblen identified as the major industrial powers of the future.[9] In any case, the experience of the Anglo-Saxon countries, where industrialism and democracy coexisted, was not likely to be repeated by late-developing countries. The story of development would be the story of divergence rather than convergence.

If one attempt at revision was made by Veblen, inspired by the experience of Germany, another was made by Lenin (1870–1924) as he pondered the practical problems of revolution in Russia, a backward country on the periphery of the modern industrial world. Here, in the course of the now familiar debate, the Menshevik wing of the Social Democratic party argued its case within the original Marxist frame of reference, pleading that before the issue of the socialist revolution could be put on the agenda, "feudal" Russia would have to pass through the developmental stages experienced by Western societies in the age of industrial capitalism. Without the full development of an industrial economy there would be no progressive and enlightened proletariat to take the lead.

As we know all too well, Lenin challenged this thesis, pointing to some fundamental differences between patterns of early and late development.[10] He correctly observed that in the West capitalism developed within the context of the agricultural and the commercial revolutions: it was in the course of these that the bourgeoisie had emerged as a class powerful enough to challenge the alliance of aristocracy and monarchy, and subsequently tó lay down the foundations of the industrial economy. Not so, however, in Russia where the industrial revolution had taken off under the auspices of the state, where the agrarian and commercial revolutions did not precede but followed the rise of an industrial economy. Here, consequently, the bourgeoisie and the proletariat would not emerge in sequence but concurrently, thereby creating conditions for a joint revolutionary venture in the course of which the industrial proletariat—absent from the revolutions of 1646 and 1789—would eventually seize the initiative and prevail. To use Lenin's own word, the two revolutions—the bourgeois and the proletarian, the liberal and the socialist—would be "telescoped" into one. Thus, instead of the two-stage process of transition characteristic of the experience of the West, late-developing societies could do it all at once, by skipping a historical stage. The paths of history would henceforth be variable: longer for the early-developing, shorter for the late-developing countries. Still, the two paths of development were expected to lead to the same ultimate stage, socialism. With these conclusions, Lenin laid down the foundations of the sequential mode of thinking about development, as well as of convergence theory.

But sequential theory and the telescoping of revolutions were not to be the last word in the debate, nor the last contribution of the Bolsheviks to political economy and sociology. For to Lenin's arguments on sequencing, opponents replied with still greater pessimism: if a revolution were to succeed by skipping stages, socialism would be saddled with the task of primary accumulation, one that history had assigned to capitalism. The process of accumulation, the Mensheviks and their allies pointed out, quoting Marx's *Capital*, required brute force that would debase the higher revolutionary purpose. Socialism in a backward society, noted Plekhanov prophetically, would result not in democracy, but in "semi-Asiatic despotism," or an "Inca empire."[11] This was powerful logic based on impeccable Marxist premises and required another rejoinder before the business of revolution could be pursued by the more radical socialists.

This rejoinder was provided by Trotsky, and then by Lenin, in separate polemic essays that provided a final rationale to the political program of Bolshevism. The essence of their arguments is well known from history books. It was, to quote Trotsky (and to paraphrase Lenin), that capitalism was a single, interdependent international phenomenon that "with its mode of production and commerce . . . has converted the whole world into a single economic and political organization."[12] Within this single organization, or system, one ought not try to separate the national and the international revolutions. The conquest of power within national limits was only to be the initial act in the revolutionary process.[13] To this thesis, Lenin provided theoretical underpinnings by pointing to "irreconcilable contradictions" among imperialist nations competing with each other for capital markets, and added his own prescription for breaking the "weakest link" in the interdependent system of imperialism.[14] The proletarian revolution, Stalin added as late as 1924, was not to be a "purely national, but an international phenomenon rooted in the whole of international development."[15] Therefore, in Leninism,

the very approach to the question of proletarian revolution, of the character of the revolution, of its scope, of its depth, the scheme of revolution in general, changes accordingly.

Formerly, the analysis of the pre-requisites of the proletarian revolution was approached from the point of view of the economic state of the individual countries. Now this approach is no longer adequate. Now the matter must be approached from the point of view of the economic state of all or the majority of countries, from the point of view of the world economy.[16]

So formulated, the theory was a powerful refutation of Menshevik arguments and the first major attempt to expand the analytic scheme of political economy beyond national political boundaries and class configurations. Alas, from the point of view of its protagonists, the global venture itself failed, and socialism was to be built in a single country. In the wake of failure, the global aspects of the theory were repressed, and the state of the art quickly regressed into the more sterile study of developmental stages. Indeed, for another 40 years or so, the idea of globalism was dead, both inside and outside Marxist scholarship. When it finally re-emerged, it did so with considerable modifications, as we shall see in Chapter 3.

The Paradigm in America: Talcott Parsons

This line of intellectual evolution, from unilinear to multilinear concepts of development, was to be repeated in the United States, a country where the study of political sociology and economy had made relatively few inroads prior to World War II—Veblen, together with George Herbert Mead and Charles Beard, representing brilliant exceptions to this generalization. This absence should not be entirely surprising. For one thing, as members of a new immigrant society, Americans were more preoccupied with changing things than with speculating about change. For another, in its splendid isolation, theirs was a special social and economic environment. Americans were a "people of plenty" to whom scarcity did not appear to be the central problem of politics. Nor was the problem of complexity as overwhelming as in the old world. For while a full-fledged industrial economy was developing in one part of the country, the individual could still retreat from industrialism into the bucolic simplicity of a vast hinterland. There, on the rural expanses of the Midwest and the West, a complex division of labor was as absent as was any formal structure of state authority: the average person could still fish and hunt in the morning, farm in the afternoon, read the scriptures at night, and all this without having been through a socialist revolution.

In this environment, economic and sociological constraints

made little sense. Public life was not so much a matter of scarcity and necessity as of virtue and institutional engineering, of finding the most appropriate set of rules for the political game. This view persisted even after the rise of a new trend of political realism, represented by Arthur Bentley before World War I and carried on by disciples like Charles Merriam and Peter Odegard in the interwar period. For although Bentley and the realists believed that the power of groups rather than formal rules were at the heart of politics, they were also more interested in the "art" of "meeting pressure with pressure" than in the changing social constraints on behavior.[17] Obviously, this particular set of interests would not engender the rise of coherent theories of political change.

Political economy and sociology arrived in a grand way only after World War II, when increasing involvement in global affairs made it imperative for both leaders and an educated public to come to grips with the source and nature of differences among political systems in various parts of the world. The response to this need was concerted and originated from the very center of the body politic. The government itself took the initiative of building up the disciplines of comparative and international studies by appropriating public revenues and, still more significantly, by encouraging private foundations to devote substantial resources for the purpose. The universities reacted favorably to the dual moral and material incentive and proceeded to build a cadre of experts, drawing heavily on the available pool of immigrant talent, above all on refugees from the formerly fascist countries.

Not surprisingly, in view of this background, the core of the discipline was built around a few continental classics of impeccable ideological credentials. Thus Durkheim and Weber emerged as the favorites of the generation, while Adam Smith was shunned, partly because continentals never quite appreciated the completeness of his social theory, partly because his liberal "orthodoxy" was seen as outmoded in this Keynesian age. Pareto, Mosca, and other sociologists of the right were definitely out: "together with Hegel, Nietzsche and a host of minor figures, they were blamed for the rise of fascism,"[18] while their theories of cycle and decay struck no sympathetic chords in a society that had an unshakeable faith in progress and development. The same faith, however, permitted Marx to reenter the discipline, if only through a back door, sanitized of his theories of exploitation and immiseration. Spencer likewise was resuscitated, but cleansed of his offensive social Darwinism.

Although immigrants loomed large in shaping the discipline, the single most important figure of the period, and the chief intermediary between European and American sociology, was a native son, albeit one who had been educated in Europe, notably in Heidelberg, the past home of Weber. Talcott Parsons (1902–79), with prodigious energy and a voracious appetite for theorizing, set out not only to bring the European classics to America, but also to weave their work into a single, overarching system. Thus Parsons's "general theory of action" was intended to accomplish nothing less than "to introduce theoretical ecumenism [into social science] on a grand scale."[19] In his own words, he set out to systematize sociology and thereby to "end the division of the field into warring 'schools' of thought."[20]

The new sociology of Parsons was to be both systematic and systemic. This is to say that, in developing his frame of reference, Parsons took significant cues from the theories of Herbert Spencer. Just like Spencer's society, Parsons's is an entity of interdependent elements that becomes a "system" by acquiring the "highest level of self-sufficiency"[21] and the capacity to respond to environmental stimuli as an integrated entity. Again, as in the theory of Spencer, the system maintains its "pattern" and its existence as a unit by performing a limited number of functions, which enable the observer to identify appropriate structures and to compare them in a systematic manner. There is, to be sure, an attempt to rid this scheme of Spencer's stultifying holism by taking into account the individual. Thus we are advised to consider "the orientations of action of *any one* given actor and its [*sic*] attendant motivational processes [as] a differentiated and integrated system. This system will be called the *personality*, and we will define it as the organized system of the orientation and motivation of action of one individual *actor*."[22] (Italics in original.) But this attempt is halfhearted and does not yield a true synthesis between a theory of the whole and a theory of the parts. To quote Parsons:

> The social system is, to be sure, made up of the relationships of individuals, but it is a system which is organized around the problems inherent in or arising from social interaction of a plurality of individual actors rather than around problems which arise in connection with the integration of the actions of an individual actor, who is also a physiological organism. Personality and social system are very intimately interrelated, but they are neither identical with one another nor explicable by one another; the social system is not a plurality of personalities.[23]

Parsons's major contributions to systems theory are twofold. First is the notion that system means interaction, that is, relationship between two or more actors. An important corollary is that in predicting social behavior of units—whether of individuals, classes, or societies—we must consider not only their own social circumstances, but also the circumstances of other actors. Behavior here is a two-way street, explained by more than a single actor's social role or status. Second, Parsons improves on Spencerian thinking by differentiating between concrete and analytic systems. While the former are social units—like the individual, the group, or society—interacting with each other, the latter are aspects of action. Specifically, Parsons distinguishes among three aspects, the social, the psychological, and the cultural.[24]

Of these three aspects of action, the social refers to features of individual and collective behavior that can be explained in reference to the division of labor, or occupational structure. "Social," here, subsumes economics and politics as "subsystems of very great strategic significance," especially in "highly differentiated societies."[25] The psychological aspect relates to behavior explicable in terms of the child's development of personality, cast in Freudian categories.[26] This conceptualization raises a number of questions. For though the relevance of these categories is obvious when it comes to individuals, they become somewhat problematic when we attempt to apply them to society at large. Assuming that Freudian categories have explanatory power, we may inquire how particular actors have resolved their childhood conflicts and then describe their psychological makeup. This, in turn, will presumably allow us to predict why the actors are responding to particular events in particular ways. But what about the psychological makeup of French, German, or Bengali society? How are we to derive them? Are we to assume that psychological conflicts are resolved in an identical manner for all actors in a given society—in which case psychology becomes redundant and should be subsumed under "culture"—or are we to create an ideal gestalt by abstracting a single order from the millions of individual cases? If so, what is the predictive value of such a prototype? Parsons is less than forthcoming with the answer, and in the absence of a clear-cut elaboration, the category merely reflects recognition of the fact that at times societies may respond irrationally, that is, in ways that cannot be reduced to either culture or self-interest.

If the psychological "subsystem" is Parsons's way to introduce the irrational into sociological analysis, the introduction of culture represents an attempt to build further on Durkheimian and Weberian categories of analysis. Drawing on more recent advances in linguistics and cultural anthropology,[27] Parsons describes culture as a "structure" and as a "symbolic system," the function of which is to organize the choices of individuals, to give them a degree of internal consistency. This is a clear-cut and helpful formula, especially when combined with the advice that culture should be approached at three different levels: the cognitive, the normative, and the expressive. However, the formula becomes more cumbersome as Parsons subsumes under the label of culture both habituated responses and conscious moral choice in response to some higher reward,[28] two categories that Weber, under the labels of traditionalism and the *Wertrational*, sharply delineated in his own system of thinking. Nor did Parsons resolve the dilemmas of Durkheim and Weber concerning either the origin of cultures or the more precise relationship of the culture to the social system. For while he tells us that "systems of culture have their own forms and problems of integration which are not reducible to those of either personality or social systems,"[29] he fails to develop the dynamics of culture formation or to provide significant clues as to the responses of different cultures to environmental "challenges." In the absence of these, the scheme amounts to little more than an elaborate taxonomy of factors that ought to be taken into consideration when we attempt to account for the responses of societies to stimuli originating from their external environment.

The ambiguities of the synthesis become still more evident if we examine Parsons's theory of social change. In this construct, too, he attempts to bring together a number of disparate elements, starting with Spencerian assumptions concerning the behavior of systems. As in Spencer's theory, change means adaptation to the exigencies of scarcity and to pressures emanating from a competitive international environment. Borrowing from Marx and Smith, Parsons tells us that societies adapt to these challenges mainly by technological innovation and "developmental breakthrough." Then, again like Spencer, he suggests that "such a breakthrough endows its society with a new level of adaptive capacity in some vital respect, thereby changing the terms of its competitive relations with other societies in the [international] system."[30] History is thus a Promethean struggle for power and against scarcity.

The changes resulting from these adaptations fall under three rubrics: (1) differentiation, familiar from the sociology of both Durkheim and Spencer; (2) integration, which

Parsons defines as political-institutional (as well as cultural) change necessitated by the disruptive consequences of differentiation; and (3) changes in value orientation, that is, in the ways in which people structure their expectations and make their fundamental choices in interacting with others. The sum of the latter appears in the well-known pattern variables, five dichotomies that describe the main direction of evolutionary change from tradition to modernity. They are (in slightly different order from the way they are presented by Parsons):[31]

1. Diffuseness–specificity.
2. Affectivity–affective neutrality.
3. Particularism–universalism.
4. Ascription–achievement.
5. Self-orientation–collectivity-orientation.

Parsons's theory of change may be approached from a number of different perspectives and may be taken to task for a number of inconsistencies. Let us start with the standard criticism that the variables are "parochial," in that they reflect no evolutionary universals, only the rather unique and idiosyncratic historical experience of the Occident. This criticism applies to Weber as well. But the Parsonian scheme is not just "Western" in orientation; it is peculiarly American in its boundless confidence in the qualities and consequences of modernity. Ironically, this has been attained by adding the fifth, essentially Marxist, category to the other four dichotomies borrowed from Weber and Durkheim. In this way, Parsons not only expands, but effectively subverts, the theory of rationalization, with its emphasis on market analogies and on the growing impersonality of social relations. In the definition of Parsons and his associates, self-orientation refers to a presumably traditionalistic frame of mind, in which it is "permissible . . . to give priority . . . to private interests . . . independently of their bearing on the interests and values of a given collectivity of which he is a member."[32] Collectivity-orientation, on the other hand, is defined as context in which the actor feels obliged "to take directly into account the value and interests of the collectivity," and "to give priority to the collective interest . . . when there is potential conflict with private interest."[33] If anything, this echoes Comte's hopes for a *sagesse universelle* or Marx's belief that socialism would restore the lost *Gemeinschaft* to industrial society. By borrowing these themes from Marx and Comte, Parsons introduces a utopian element into his theory and transforms the darkest forebodings of Durkheim and Weber into an exuberant optimism.

But the scheme has further, and perhaps still graver, problems that stem from Parsons's failure to provide logical links among the different layers of the theory. The nexus between technology and differentiation, to be sure, is clear enough and has been recognized by social scientists since the beginning of the industrial age. But the nexus between differentiation and integration is more difficult to discern, especially because "integration" here means both political institutionalization and the creation of new cultural norms appropriate to a changing social structure. Both of these forms of adaptation raise the age-old questions of how, when, and why. And what about the pattern variables? In Weber's thinking, the loss of affect and the emphasis on impersonality and achievement reflect market analogies and are related to the capitalist mode of *exchange*. As such they provide a picture of modernity qua capitalism. But Parsons identifies these with "industrial societies," and with the mode of *production*, thereby confusing a generation of social scientists about the possible distinctions between the two.

Further ambiguities arise from the way in which Parsons attempts to explain the relationship between the pattern variables and the cultural system. For the variables are alternatively described as culture in change or as change mediated, or caused, by the cultural system. In *The Social System* Parsons describes them as "patterns of articulation between the cultural orientation system and the other components of action,"[34] but in *Toward a General Theory* they "become relevant at different levels"; they are "inherently patterns of cultural value orientation."[35] They are also described as "habits of choice," and as such, "a bit of internalized culture."[36] They "enter on the cultural level as aspects of value standards"; or "they perform different functions for different analytic systems: culturally they define patterns of value orientation."[37]

In retrospect, it is difficult to ascertain whether the problem was purely semantic or semantic and conceptual. In either case, Parsons's lack of clarity in definitions became a major factor in the collapse of causality in the new theory of modernization. While classical sociologists and economists were able to define their subject matter in a crisp and clear fashion, the neo-classical universe became a complex maze of variables in which everything was related to everything else, and the disparate elements of the changing social system hung together, not on grounds of logic, but of a higher and occasionally mythical necessity. Without further belaboring the point, we may illustrate this by quoting Daniel Lerner's formula of modernization, which in turn has been widely quoted and adapted by others as an introduction to the subject matter. According to Lerner, modernization is

a process with some distinctive *quality* of its own, which would explain why modernity is felt as a *consistent whole* among people who live by its rules. We know that urbanization, industrialization, secularization, democratization, education, media participation do not occur in a haphazard and unrelated fashion, even though we are often obliged to study them singly. Our multiple correlations . . . have shown them to be so highly associated as to raise the question whether they are genuinely independent factors at all—suggesting that perhaps they went together so regularly, because, in some sense, they *had* to go together.[38] (Italics in original.)

Theories of Modernization and Development

Whatever its internal contradictions and inconsistencies, Parsons's attempt at a modern synthesis of classical theories had considerable influence on his students and contemporaries. For a younger generation of social scientists just returning from a long war and in a hurry to enter the discipline, there was often too little time for immersion in the great classics of European sociology. But whereas not all members of this generation acquired profound knowledge of Durkheim, Spencer, or Weber, all of them had a chance to read Parsons, and it was through him that many became acquainted with functionalism, or with the concepts of differentiation and rationalization (in Parsonian language, value orientation), which then became the cornerstones of a new political sociology of modernization and development.[39]

One of the most comprehensive elaborations of these concepts is to be found in the successive theoretical and empirical studies of Marion J. Levy Jr.[40] The major themes of these studies are well within the Parsonian frame of reference. They include the concepts of both structure and function, and they deal with processes of change in the division of labor that originate in technological change. The concept of function is universal and includes a finite number of conditions, "in the absence of which the termination of society would result."[41] The list of these functions, or alternatively, "functional requisites,"[42] is, in Levy's own opinion, neither particularly novel nor counterintuitive from the point of view of the standard sociological works of the time.[43] It includes provisions for recruitment ("role assignment and role differentiation"), socialization, communication, acculturation ("shared cognitive orientations"), controls of disruptive behavior, and adequate institutionalization.[44] But the view of society in the process of differentiation and the concept of function together permit Levy in his later work to make effective comparisons among different types, as well as predictions concerning structures and institutional changes in modernizing societies.[45] The more complex the society, the more involved the structures are in the performance of particular functions. This feature of the theory made it popular in its own time, especially, as we shall see subsequently, among students of comparative politics interested in bridging the analytic gap between the "advanced societies" of the Occident, and the "developing societies" of the Third World.

The concept of differentiation also plays a key role in Neil Smelser's study of the industrial revolution and the development of the British cotton industry in the eighteenth century.[46] But differentiation here does not mean straight ascent to the heaven of modernity. It rather means a process of transition from one equilibrium stage to another. The intellectual rationale of his study is to demonstrate that the process of change from less to more differentiated societies "possesses definite regularities," that differentiation is "set in motion by specific disequilibrating conditions," and that change can only proceed further if the resultant "disturbances" are "brought in line by specific integrative measures."[47] Indeed, the element of "disturbance," or strain, is so important that we no longer deal with a strict dichotomy, but with a three-stage model, from the equilibrium of tradition to the disequilibrium of transition, and then back again to the equilibrium of modernity. This general proposition is then verified, or illustrated, by tracing the path of change from technological innovation to structural differentiation in spinning and weaving and, further, to pressures on the division of labor in the family. From these pressures, the author takes us to symptoms of disturbance in the family and, finally, to the response of society by a variety of integrative measures: labor legislation, the establishment of trade unions, the founding of "friendly societies" and cooperative organizations.

The three-stage model of social change is still more explicit in Fred Riggs's *Administration in Developing Countries*.[48] Following closely in the footsteps of Parsons, Riggs describes social change in part as differentiation, in part as transition from traditionalism to modernity. To designate these well-known types, he creates his own terminology. Thus traditional societies become "fused," differentiation becomes "diffraction," and modern society is a "diffracted society."[49] However, unlike other writers before him, Riggs does not regard transitional society as disequilibrated society or as a mixture of traditional and modern elements, but as a stage of development that has "its own peculiar logic,"[50] and must be understood in its own terms. To label this intermediate stage, Riggs coined the term "prismatic,"[51] derived from the metaphor of light passing through a prism.

This prismatism has several facets. In economics it refers neither to traditional pricing by fiat nor to modern pricing by the market mechanism, but to a state of "price indeterminacy,"[52] which explains the seemingly endless haggling between buyers and sellers in the prismatic marketplace. In the realm of administration it refers neither to the dominance of clans nor to the prevalence of meritocratic elites, but to the preeminence of "clects," recruited by "attainment,"[53] that is, by applying meritocratic principles, but only within the narrow, particularistic confines of groups defined by ethnic or other hereditary criteria. The structure of authority in these prismatic societies is neither hierarchical nor pluralistic, but "bureaucratic"; while parliamentary institutions exist, their membership is subject to administrative controls exercised through various forms of electoral engineering. Likewise, social behavior is not typically agrarian or industrial. People, Riggs notes, are not indifferent to the value of time, but neither are they inclined to allocate it rationally. Rather, "increasing economic interdependence causes many to live in a maelstrom of frantic activity. Inadequate scheduling of time leads to alternate periods of underoccupation and furies of last minute work to meet urgent deadlines."[54] As with other members of the school, with Riggs the transitional stage of the "prismatic society" is a stepping stone to better things and a preliminary to a "diffracted" modern world. Riggs does, however, admonish that "there is no reason why transitional societies should succeed in their efforts to become modern, nor is it inevitable that the remaining traditional systems should become transitional or modern."[55]

If Levy, Smelser, and Riggs focus their attention on the

causes and consequences of differentiation, another group
of Parsons's disciples pivot their analyses around changing
value orientations and the psychological dimensions of social
change. Three authors are especially noteworthy here. One is
Daniel Lerner, whose study of modernization examines "the
infusion of the rationalist and positivist spirit"[56] of the West
into the traditional societies of the Middle East. The purpose
of Lerner's study is to show that "the Western model of modernization exhibits certain components and sequences whose
relevance is global," and that "the same basic model reappears
in virtually all modernizing societies in all continents of the
world."[57] The result of this "infusion" is a new type of "mobile"
personality, or "modern man," characterized by empathy and
a high capacity for identification with new aspects of his environment.[58] But the infusion of new values and orientations is
also a source of psychological strain, arising out of two circumstances. First, the infusion of Western images creates "persons
imbued by aspirations for a future which will be better than
the past, but [these persons] have not yet acquired a comprehensive set of new values to replace the old, [and hence] they
exhibit ambivalent feelings."[59] Second, although some of these
aspirations can be fulfilled, others cannot, which leads to a
deep sense of frustration and anger. This is especially salient
in politics, where one new aspiration is to "participate," but existing political institutions do not provide appropriate partici-
patory outlets and opportunities.[60]

The other writers, Karl Deutsch and Alex Inkeles (with his
collaborator David Smith),[61] likewise direct our attention to
changing value orientations and the cognitive aspects of
change, juxtaposing habit with deliberate choice as the chief
defining characteristics of tradition and modernity. Inkeles
and Smith are concerned with the growing "cognitive openness" of "modern man," and they treat modernization as a
process of increasing receptivity to new ideas and social diversity. For Deutsch, the key aspect of modernization is the "mobilization" of populations in reference to their "availability for

recommitment," a concept that echoes not only Weber's rationalization, but Marx's concept of social consciousness and
Mannheim's idea of "fundamental democratization" as well.[62]
As traditional social structures disintegrate, and as former
"traditionals" become drawn into the modern world by markets and educational systems, they "enter" the political process
as active participants. Both Deutsch and Inkeles cast their theories in rather narrow sociological frameworks: changes in
perception and habits of choice closely follow economic innovations and transformations in the social structure. For Inkeles and Smith the factory is the most effective "school of modernity." In Deutsch's seminal article mobilization is related to
a broad spectrum of variables—education, industrialization,
media exposure, market relations—within which, once again,
relationships between cause and effect are less than clear-cut.

Still more ambitious attempts to apply Parsonian categories
to empirical analysis were made by a number of political scientists who not only tried to grasp the dynamics of change in
"developing" countries, but also set out to create a single, comprehensive frame of reference for the comparative study of
Western and non-Western political systems. The most important of these political scientists is Gabriel A. Almond who, with
a number of collaborators, produced a series of volumes to accomplish the larger theoretical purpose. In *The Politics of the
Developing Areas*, coedited with James S. Coleman, Almond
narrows the Parsonian concept of politics to those aspects of
integration that involve the employment of "more or less
legitimate physical compulsion,"[63] and from this narrower
definition of the subject matter emerge his seven political
functions: rule making, enforcement, adjudication, political
recruitment, socialization, communication, interest articulation, and interest aggregation.[64] The case studies in the volume are intended to demonstrate how the performance of
these functions changes as a result of differentiation and
structural change. But this objective is only partly accomplished, because the volume addresses only the experience of

"developing" areas, with no attempt to contrast it with patterns prevalent in Communist or Western industrial states. Apart from differentiation, Almond and his associates were also concerned with the cultural dimensions of change. At first, in *The Politics of the Developing Areas*, this category is treated as "secularization," in reference to changes from traditionalism to a more rationalized system of value orientations.[65] So defined, secularization and differentiation go together, and cultural change is merely another dimension of the overall process of modernization. In a later volume, coauthored by Almond and G. Bingham Powell, this aspect of the theory became modified by redefining culture in a more conventional manner as the sum total of "attitudes, beliefs and feelings about politics . . . shaped by the nation's history."[66] In this formulation, culture, rather than being part of the overall process of change, can now explain modernization and its historical variability, even though some ambiguity continues to linger as the authors insist that culture is also molded by "ongoing processes of social, economic, and political activity."[67]

In a somewhat similar vein, another political scientist, David Apter, addresses the problems of differentiation and changing value orientations in his *Politics of Modernization*. Writing in the best Parsonian tradition and well within the premises of the neo-classical paradigm, Apter relates his subject to the "twin processes of commercialization and industrialization," though he also suggests that "in many non-Western areas, modernization has been a result of commercialization and, rather than industrialization, bureaucracy."[68] Apter's main purpose is to examine the empirical, the normative, and the strategic implications of the process of modernization and, further, to summarize the existing state of knowledge at the time of his writing. He does succeed in the latter enterprise, but like most Parsonians he is dogged by the problem of definition and fails to untangle the complex web of causality. Thus while industrialization is described as the *cause* of modernization in the West, it is also described as one of the effects of modernization in non-Western countries.[69] The argument becomes tangled when we encounter the concept of "development," which is described as the *result* of the "proliferation and integration of functional roles in a community."[70] Matters do not become easier when we learn that modernization is a "particular case of development," in that it "implies three conditions—a social system that can constantly innovate without falling apart; differentiated, flexible social structures; and a social framework to provide the skills and knowledge necessary for living in a technologically advanced world."[71]

Whatever their precise meaning, these definitions of modernization and development evoke the Spencerian image of a differentiated society, that is, one that possesses vastly superior capabilities for dealing with the challenges of the environment. However, Apter, whose empirical work on African countries shows Weber's influence, is far less certain than Spencer or Parsons that modern societies will be democratic as well. Indeed, at one point in his book on modernization, he seems to share the darkest forebodings of Weber and Durkheim that, "having lost its religious basis, our society is in danger of becoming a system of organized plunder."[72] Overall, Apter's work is far more eclectic and tentative than Almond's, and while it is full of challenging insights, it also conveys a sense that his conclusions might soon be overtaken by new developments in this fragile and rapidly changing field. In his own words, his are "theories for burning."[73]

Although American social science was dominated by Parsonians during the first two decades of the postwar period, not all social scientists were Parsonians. One alternative school tended to focus its attention, not on structure or on value configurations, but on scarcity and the gratification of material needs. One example for this mode of thinking may be found in Seymour M. Lipset's *Political Man*,[74] a volume of essays that owes as much to the great economic theorists of history as to Max Weber, whose concept of politics dominates the work. Following Weber, Lipset suggests that the stability of any political order depends on two factors, expediency and legitimacy. The former can be explained mainly by the ability of a regime to satisfy the material aspirations of the population. Legitimacy is a more complex matter. Its roots may be in culture and history, in the collective memories of the population. Political change, then, is related to changes in these categories.

In practical terms, however, levels of scarcity and abundance seem to be of decisive importance. Such, at least, is the conclusion that we can draw from Lipset's observation that "the most common generalization linking political systems to other aspects of society has been that democracy is related to the state of economic development."[75] To test the hypothesis "concretely," Lipset uses various indexes of economic development and finds close correlations between per capita income, industrialization, urbanization, and education on the one hand, and the "degree" of stable democracy on the other. On his scale, "European and English-speaking stable democracies" have twice as much income per capita as do "European unstable democracies"; Latin American "democracies and unstable dictatorships" outrank "stable dictatorships" by about 65 percent.[76] There are also shades here of the old Spencerian agraria-industria hypothesis: "The average percentage of employed males in agriculture and related occupations was 21 in the 'more democratic' European countries and 41 in the 'less democratic.'"[77] There are no fixed thresholds in this scheme, but its implications are clear: political progress equals democratization, and democratization requires a steady increase of material abundance.

Another work, published like Lipset's in 1960, is Walt W. Rostow's more elaborate, and in its own time highly popular, *The Stages of Economic Growth.*[78] In this "anti-Communist Manifesto," as he called it, the writer borrows a number of key elements from Marx, above all the concept of stages defined in economic terms. As in Marx's theory, all societies are likely to pass through five stages in history. For Rostow these are tradition, preconditions, takeoff, drive to maturity, and mass consumption. Though liberal and anti-Marxist in tone, the final stage is described in the same utopian terms as Marx's socialism. Here, however, social peace is not the result of equality but of abundance that is seen to reduce political conflict to manageable proportions. Unlike Marx, who could only point to the future when describing socialism, Rostow can also point to the present, above all, to the United States and its European allies, with a few others close to the threshold of ultimate fulfillment.

No less sweeping than Rostow's *Stages of Economic Growth* is Cyril Black's *Dynamics of Modernization*. This work is neither strictly sociological nor economic in orientation and, for want of a better term, may be described as a political approach to comparative history. This label is justified by Black's emphasis on political power, institutions, and leadership, which he identifies as requisites for the survival of societies in a competitive world. Unlike the works of Levy and Almond (Black's one-time colleagues at Princeton), *The Dynamics of Modernization* is not overtly Parsonian in orientation, but it has an unmistakably functionalist flavor in developing its argument. In order to compete effectively with rivals, societies must "respond to four critical problems that all modernizing societies must face: 1) the challenge of modernity—the initial confrontation of society . . . with modern ideas and institutions; . . . 2) the consolidating of modernizing leadership; 3) economic and social transformation; . . . 4) the integration of society."[79] It is in terms of these challenges that Black distinguishes among four stages of development in the modern history of societies, and he then proceeds to compare the progress of 155 countries. By 1966, fourteen had achieved the highest stage of development; nineteen had yet to enter the first. The others, among them Soviet Russia, fell between these two extremes, but in any case, were seen to occupy a far lower rung on the developmental ladder than the United States.[80]

Much like Rostow's *Stages of Growth*, *The Dynamics of Modernization* is essentially an optimistic work. In Black's words:

the end is not easy to foresee, but as automation reduces the labor force required to sustain economic growth, it is not unlikely that a substantial proportion of the work force of an integrated society will be guaranteed an income regardless of whether or not they work. Under these conditions a radical redistribution of employment and leisure becomes normal. . . . When societies reach this phase there is also much greater consensus among interest groups regarding the policies of modernization that should be followed. Conservatives, liberals, and socialists still engage in lively political struggles, but differences in policy regarding major issues are greatly reduced.[81]

If so, not only the Asian and African states, but the totalitarian states of East Europe as well, might look forward to a much brighter future.

Transitional Society: One Road or Many?

The theories of Parsons and those of the first generation of Parsonians were not only evolutionist in character, they were very strict in their interpretation of evolution and progress. This is to say that most members of the immediate postwar period were inclined to see modernization either as an ascent on the ladder of differentiation and prosperity or as passage across the bridge over the "great dichotomy,"[82] in the course of which societies would follow the same political and social patterns. Progress, to be sure, could exact a certain price. But as in the *Pilgrim's Progress*, virtuous suffering would reap its eventual reward. Much like Bunyan's pilgrim, whose peregrinations through the wilderness were fraught with temptations and perils, developing societies would eventually negotiate their way through the Valley of Despair and gain entry through the Shining Gates of modernity.

The road, though, would always be the same. Intellectually, the emphasis was on similarity, to the point where highly disparate political events were construed to be the instances of the same general historical phenomenon. Revolutions, coups d'état, and endemic violence in Third World societies thus were often seen as historical equivalents of the upheaval that followed the commercial, agricultural, and industrial revolutions of Western Europe and Britain. Transition meant political trouble, and conversely, where there was political trouble, it was easily attributed to the dislocations and strains of transition. It was in this vein that at one time Parsons described Italian and German Fascism as the symptoms of transition, "at least as deeply rooted in the social structure and the dynamics of our society [in change] as was socialism at an earlier stage."[83]

Strict evolutionism and the unilinear view of modernization, however, were to be passing phenomena, for a good number of social scientists felt considerable unease about attempts to fit contemporary experiences into the categories of an essentially historical model. It was one thing to speculate in the abstract that the countries of the Second and Third World were in the process of transition, and another to argue that specific contemporary phenomena—totalitarian purges, concentration camps, military coups—were somehow the historical equivalents of the nineteenth-century experience of Britain and the European countries. Thus, upon some reflection, in time a new general hypothesis and mode of thinking emerged, arguing that in the study of modernization we should expect to discover, not one, but two or more paths or patterns of development. One of these paths can be traced back by examining the historical experience of the "pioneering," or early-developing, countries, the others by studying the current experience of the late-developing countries (or LDC's, as the countries of the Third World came to be known in the new terminology of the early 1960's). This new mode of thinking was reminiscent of the theories of Lenin and Veblen, except that the new revisionists saw "late development" not so much a historical advantage as a disadvantage, that is, as a condition that in and of itself would be a source of strain. Late developers, in other words, would have to pay a much higher price for progress and travel a rockier road to progress than did their "advanced," or early-developing, brethren.

The explanations for the extra strain varied, and these variations allow us to distinguish among different types of neo-evolutionist thinking. The most popular of these explanations emerged from a work somewhat extraneous to the general literature on development—Isaac Deutscher's study of Stalinism.[84] Deutscher's themes were then further elaborated by economists like Karl deSchweinitz, Robert Heilbroner, Alexander Gerschenkron, and by David Apter, who in one of his earlier essays adopted this mode of analysis to explain variations in the political structures of new African states.[85] The essence of this economic theory is that backward societies, under pressure to "catch up," need to accumulate large amounts of capital within a relatively short span of time and from economies that have a very low capacity to generate voluntary savings. Confronted with this need, backward societies will have to gear their institutions to the task of mobilizing manpower and scarce resources for development. While this task can be accomplished in a number of ways, the most efficient way is to create a "mobilization system" (Apter) with highly coercive institutions and with a "consummatory" utopian ideology capable of justifying the need for human sacrifice in terms of salvationist prophesies and higher historical purposes. If this picture is bleak, it is brightened by the prospect that these mobilization regimes will not have to be relied on forever. For once the "hump" of accumulation (deSchweinitz) has been overcome, the need for coercion will progressively decline to permit the rise of more tolerant and pluralistic "reconciliation systems" (Apter). By the same logic Deutscher had successfully predicted the decline of terror and arbitrary government in the Soviet Union. The validity of the theory was thus seemingly verified both by the multiplication of repressive one-party regimes in the Third World and by the deradicalization of European Communist regimes. Thus, in the public realm the theory emerged as a major intellectual rationale for a two-pronged foreign policy, one that advocated detente with a "post-revolutionary" Soviet Union and indulgence toward friendly, but internally repressive, Third World regimes.

A particularly sophisticated version of this theory is to be found in Alexander Gerschenkron's now famous article "Economic Backwardness in Historical Perspective."[86] Written with the intent of challenging the classical evolutionist view that backward societies may be expected to follow in the footsteps of the pioneering nations, the article points not only to typical contrasts between early- and late-developing countries, but also to more subtle variations due to "timing" or to the degree of relative backwardness with which a given society enters the industrial age. Like Heilbroner, deSchweinitz, and others whom he inspired, Gerschenkron sees as the pivotal issue the manner in which investments are financed in the rising industrial economy. If in pioneering England the industrial economy was largely the product of individual entrepreneurship and of cycles of savings and reinvestment, in the countries of the European continent the strains of relative backwardness and the urgency and pressures for catching up with England necessitated specialized economic institutions—the large holding banks of modern finance capitalism. In still more backward Russia the task of mobilizing savings could only be performed by the public sector, that is, by potentially coercive institutions of the state.

These variations in the manner of the primary accumulation of capital in turn provide some insights into differences in the structure of state institutions and public authority. In England, political democracy seemed to be a natural corollary of a system of voluntary savings. In Germany and France, powerful and politically autonomous bureaucracies were needed to protect the large concentrations of capital generated by the banking system. In Russia, meanwhile, development required an all-powerful state capable of extorting surplus from a society that could generate no savings by means of the market mechanism. So formulated, the historical argument provides us with a hypothesis by analogy concerning the political future of still more backward societies. It also raises a renewed challenge to Veblen's hypothesis concerning the potential advantages of economic backwardness.

Whereas the political economists have developed their arguments in terms of excessive demands on scarce resources, political sociologists, including some of the Parsonians, make their case in terms of different degrees of cultural change and social disjuncture. Most of these writers make distinctions between the "endogenous" social change of the Occident and the "exogenous" changes we encounter in the late-developing countries. If in the West the problem was transition, in the non-Western countries the problem is compounded by alien cultural and institutional patterns. The distinction is not always sharply made, but is evident upon closer examination. Thus Riggs's "prismatism" involves not only transition from tradition to modernity, but confrontation between the Western structures of bureaucracy and the cultural norms of a non-Western society as well. Likewise, Lerner saw strain as the product of a disequilibrium not merely between traditional structure and modern aspirations, but also between local structure and alien aspirations, embodied in the "positivist and rationalist spirit of the West."[87] This is a critical difference, which suggests some explanations of why his transitionals submit so readily to the lures of radical mass movements and charismatic politics.

Different Roads and Different Outcomes

In retrospect, the model of a transitional society and the concept of "different roads" represented a definite advance over the strict evolutionism of earlier days. The revision of the theory added new dimensions to comparative politics and generated a new agenda for research. Instead of the sterile search for stages, it steered scholarship toward the search for "substitutes" (Gerschenkron) and alternative strategies, and on the whole toward more systematic explanations of diversity.

Nevertheless, this was not a radical departure from earlier premises, and the epistemological continuities between the old theory and the new were just as important as the elements of change. For one thing, the explanations were still largely formulated in terms of "timing," that is, the chronological point of departure from traditionalism. For another, the fundamental assumptions of the theory remained teleological and highly optimistic. Although the LDC's were expected to pay a higher price for progress than the pioneering societies, they were still expected to "catch up" with the advanced societies and to reach a common terminal point of balanced modernity.

This optimistic mood, however, was gradually dissipated by the cumulative experience of two postwar decades, the obvious absence of economic progress in too many "new nations," and the equally obvious spread of revolutionary movements and authoritarian regimes. These experiences tended to cast doubt on the idea of universal progress and spurred yet another revisionist movement among American social scientists of the mainstream. As part of this movement, some social scientists of the 1960's were no longer content to map out different roads and strategies of transition, but began to contemplate the possibility of radically different historical outcomes that would stay with us in the modern world. Most significantly, political scientists began to ponder the prospects of democracy as well as dictatorship in modern society, and made it their first priority to identify the "roots," or causes, of these alternative results of development. (These and the other changes in the theory of modernization are summarized in Table 1.)

One of these attempts to explain different historical outcomes was made by Lucian W. Pye, whose theory was cast in a sequential mold and as such recalls the idea of "telescoping" developments, prevalent in the old Marxist debate about the politics of backward societies. Pye's concept of development, to be sure, had little in common with the Marxist view of history. Rather, the theory was cast implicitly in a functionalist mold, in that it rested on the assumption that modernization (or, alternatively, nation-building or political development) re-

TABLE 1
Theories of Modernization and Development

| | EPISTEMOLOGY | | | |
| | Strict evolutionism | Transitional society: convergence | | Different outcomes |
ORGANIZING CONCEPT		unilinear	multilinear	
Sociological: Differentiation Value orientation	Parsons (early) Inkeles-Smith Almond-Coleman	Parsons (late) Apter (*Modernization*) Deutsch	Lerner[a] Riggs	Almond-Powell Bendix
Economic: Scarcity Accumulation	Rostow	Lipset (*Political Man*)	Gerschenkron Deutscher Heilbroner deSchweinitz Apter ("System, Process")	Huntington
Historical: Adaptation sequences			Black[a]	Pye B. Moore

[a]Implicit in analysis.

quired the performance of a finite number of historical tasks: the building of a rationalized system of public administration, the more equitable distribution of social resources, the institutionalization of political participation, the administrative penetration of rural areas, the development of a modern economic infrastructure and network of communications, the creation of a sense of national solidarity, and so on.[88] Differences in historical outcomes would then be explained by the order in which these tasks are approached and by the success or failure of modernizing elites to deal with the attendant developmental "crises." Should, for instance, the crises of distribution and penetration be successfully resolved before the crisis of participation, the society is likely to become a stable democracy. Should the sequencing be reversed, the prospects are not for democracy, but for authoritarianism or totalitarianism. While on the surface deductive, in reality this functionalist scheme has been derived a posteriori from comparisons between the Western past and the troubled present of non-Western societies.

Another significant attempt to explain different political outcomes is made by Barrington Moore in his magisterial study *The Social Origins of Dictatorship and Democracy*.[89] This study owes as much to Marx's economic class analysis of politics as it does to R. H. Tawney's idea that the agricultural revolution of the countryside, rather than the industrial revolution of the cities, holds the key to the success of modern capitalism and parliamentarism.[90] But by successfully synthesizing these two intellectual strands, Moore emerges as a theorist in his own right, transcending both Tawney's narrower concerns with the agrarian gentry, and Marx's strictly deterministic view of the historical process.

Moore's historical explanations must be approached at two separate levels. At the first level, political outcomes—democracy or dictatorship—are explained by social configurations and political coalitions. The agrarian entrepreneur and the urban bourgeois together are likely to strive for democracy; the traditional seigneur allied to the industrialist will be a coalition for fascism. But these class configurations themselves are explained by two contingencies, in turn the products of historical accident: the commercial transformation of the agrarian economy and the occurrence, or incidence, of violent revolution to eradicate the vestiges of old regimes. Out of the possible combinations of these contingencies there arise four possible paths to modernity: commercialization and revolution together breed democracy; commercialization without revolution results in fascism; revolution without commercialization leads to communist revolutions, and finally, the absence of both commercialization and revolution is the harbinger of political stagnation and decay.

Unfortunately, this ingenious scheme is buried under an enormous volume of historical detail and suffers from the author's tendency to devote an inordinate amount of effort to elaborating marginal differences among cases of the same type. There is, for instance, an overly detailed discussion of the differences in the degree and kind of commercial impulse experienced by France and England, almost obscuring the fact that these seemingly divergent examples are used to develop the same general case, that of democratic transformation. There is also a somewhat summary discussion of cultural factors to explain both marginal and substantial differences among the divergent cases, and these explanations coexist uneasily with historical accident, which is freely invoked whenever there is too much tension between history and the theory. Some two decades after its 1966 publication, readers of the volume are likely to object to its strictly reductionist approach to politics and to its failure to recognize the autonomy of the state or the importance of such political entities as the German and the Russian bureaucracies. Still, partly because of Moore's attempt to justify revolution as an instrument of progress, partly because of the sheer scope of the intellectual endeavor, Moore's volume was perhaps the single most popular work written by a social scientist in the 1960's.

Another and no less significant contribution to this branch of developmental thinking and historical sociology comes from Reinhard Bendix. Whereas Moore borrowed his leitmotifs from Tawney and Marx, Bendix's debt is to Veblen, whose methods of analysis he carries forward in his study *Nation-Building and Citizenship.*[91] Like Veblen, Bendix makes a strong case for the importance of understanding the durability of social configurations and cultural patterns, and in these terms he offers explanations as to why, in the age of industrialism, some societies turn out to be pluralistic democracies and others become autocracies. The most critical factor here appears to be the prevalence of a tradition of legalism, reciprocal restraint, and *pouvoirs intermédiaires* poised between the individual and the state. But Bendix's analysis goes beyond Veblen. Writing two world wars and several totalitarian experiments later, Bendix does not share Veblen's disdain for Britain nor his dark forebodings of English economic and political decay. In addition, he refuses to accept Veblen's thesis concerning the advantages inherent in backwardness. Indeed, he makes the very opposite case. Backwardness is a burden, and in some instances backwardness and the need to catch up will conspire with the absence of a legalistic tradition to produce authoritarian government and a highly restrictive form of citizenship.

Bendix's work is noteworthy, not only because of its unique ability to strike a balance between continuity and change, but also because of its sensitivity toward some of the shortcomings of neo-classicist theories of modernization and development. Thus in an article published in 1967 and subsequently republished in the second edition of *Nation-Building and Citizenship*,[92] he remonstrates against the tendency among his peers to treat societies as "natural systems" and to assume that industrialization will have the same effects wherever it occurs.[93] Instead of a narrow focus on the social division of labor, Bendix urges all to "attend to the external setting of society,"[94] and proposes a "reorientation" of the discipline that "considers the industrialization and democratization of Europe a singular historical breakthrough, culminating in a century-long and specifically European development. But [this] modernization brings about special discontinuities so that the relationship between the intrinsic structure and external setting of societies assumes special significance."[95] There is here as yet no alternative grand theory. But by recognizing the limits of the classical concept of an equilibrated, self-maintaining system, Bendix anticipates the new wave of developments in the 1970's and 1980's.

While Moore and Bendix concerned themselves with the kind of government that modern industrial societies are likely to evolve, Samuel P. Huntington, the author of yet another influential volume, *Political Order in Changing Societies*, was more concerned with political institutionalization and effectiveness—in his own words, with the "degree of government."[96] Indeed, Huntington's concept of "development" is not social or economic but political in character. It refers to the successful institutionalization of a system of public authority. Still, his analysis is two-pronged. Where Moore and Bendix take the worldwide progress of industrialism more or less for granted, Huntington is not only interested in political stability but also in the success or failure of economic modernization. In discussing the latter, Huntington reverts to the realism of Adam Smith and Spencer by suggesting that not all presently underdeveloped countries will ever be able to develop a viable industrial economy. The explanations for success and failure are, by Huntington's own admission, somewhat ambiguously stated, for which he has been subjected to persistent criticism.[97] Still, the direction of the argument is clear: while economic development in and by itself is not sufficient to guarantee political development, its failure will be the principal source of "political decay" and of the rise of "praetorianism," a kind of Hobbesian war of all against all, punctuated by periodic military coups d'état and dictatorship.[98]

THREE

Breakthrough: From the Social to the Global System

Neo-Classicism: A Balance Sheet

Looking back at this body of social science, we have to conclude that even from the vantage point of a critically minded decade, the various attempts to adapt nineteenth-century theory to twentieth-century realities have contributed perceptibly to the understanding of diversity in our larger, worldwide political environment. For one thing, these attempts, especially when harnessed to the American proclivity for empiricism, did stimulate research that had illuminating results, irrespective of the philosophical underpinnings of theory. For example, Riggs's study of "prismatism" remains a landmark in the portrayal of politics and markets in non-Western countries, whether they are following a given path from tradition to modernity or not. Similarly, Barrington Moore's conclusions concerning the consequences of failed agricultural revolutions are valid whether or not the underlying assumptions concerning modernization are justifiable within the context of a general theory of politics.

Still, having been built on the assumptions of the classical paradigm, modernization theory and developmental thinking have continued to display some of that paradigm's basic flaws. First, even when they acknowledged the potential for stagnation and nondevelopment, the theories showed a strong teleological bent by positing the existence of an ultimate stage of development, that of modern industrialism. Worse still, the theories did so without providing adequate thresholds to indicate when societies attain critical levels of maturity. This should not be entirely surprising: differentiation, rationalization, mobilization, and economic development are, after all, essentially open-ended processes. In the absence of obvious and a priori discernable thresholds, the tendency was either to assign totally arbitrary numerical indexes—in terms of per capita income, literacy, or the size of the nonagricultural labor force—to developmental stages or to conclude that certain political outcomes, such as the rise of an effectively functioning party system, were the signs of maturity and modernity. In this manner, in the 1950's and 1960's a number of European countries, among them Italy, Spain, and Austria, were reclassified as advanced industrial, notwithstanding the fact that their social and economic structure continued to display numerous "traditional" or preindustrial elements. At the same time, Communist societies have continued to pose a special problem, and to this date no consensus has emerged as to whether they are "developing," "developed," or a class of societies that should be treated totally in its own terms, outside any developmental frame of reference.

Another and perhaps still more crucial point of criticism arises out of what may be called the structural parochialism of conventional political sociology. This parochialism is expressed in a tendency to seek explanations for political phenomena solely within the structure and culture of the "underlying" society. In this mode of analysis French politics is explained by French culture, German politics by configurations among social classes in Germany, Russian politics by the mode of production in Russia, and so on. This is not to say that neo-classical scholarship was oblivious to exogenous sources of change. Indeed, writers like Barrington Moore and Gerschenkron repeatedly remind us of their importance, while others, like

Riggs[1] and John Kautsky, build their models around the very dichotomy of "modernization from within and modernization from without."[2] They all recognize that in most contemporary instances the impulse for economic development is provided by the past experience of the "pioneering" Western countries. But when they do so, with a handful of exceptions,[3] they interpose the social structure between the exogenous impulse and the dependent variable of politics. Thus although modernization may come from within or from without, even when it comes from without, it is seen to "work itself out" by transforming the division of labor, the social structure, or the distribution of social resources.

The Western impact on non-Western society has thus been seen to operate through the industrialization and commercialization of the host country or through the introduction of a new bureaucracy and educational system, which in turn are seen as the producers of new attitudes and interests. Altogether, within the neo-classical model "societal" changes remain the immediate causes of political change, and, conversely, there is no political change without "societal" change. This mode of thinking—eminently Durkheimian, but not alien to Marx either—has led many a scholar to conclude, much in the manner of medieval scholasticism, that whenever we encounter a polity in turmoil or change, an explanation must be found in some disturbance within the social or economic system.

Upon sober reflection we may conclude that this structural parochialism really stems from misusing the analogies drawn from the British and early European experience. This is to say that the "societal" mode of analysis is quite an appropriate explanation of political change, say, in eighteenth- or nineteenth-century Britain. There a factory was built on the edge of a village, then another, and yet another. The factory would transform peasants into workers; it would change the division of labor in society. A great number of factories would turn villages into cities, whose inhabitants would acquire new perspectives and a new political weight which they would eventually bring to bear upon the political process. Political reform or revolution might follow. In either case the path between economic cause and political effect, however tortuous, will be obvious. But take the case of Chad, Mali, Upper Volta, or dozens of other "emerging" countries. There the problem is not socio-economic change but stagnation and the absence of change. It is not that too many factories have been built and have disrupted the traditional social structure. Rather too few have been built to be able to satisfy rising expectations. At the same time political change may be endemic: a parliamentary system may be replaced by a one-party state, party politicians may be evicted by military leaders, or coup d'état may simply follow coup d'état. Here, too, we may conceptualize politics and political consciousness as part of a "superstructure." But where in the social structure can we locate a "base" on which political authority and consciousness may be said to rest?

Paradigm Crisis

Needless to say, the old paradigm was not helpful in dealing with this anomaly, and this inability became the source of a growing sense of malaise in the discipline. Among the symptoms of the crisis were the already mentioned problems of definition and causality and the growing opaqueness of the language, accompanied by a creeping sense that the theories formulated from the existing paradigm were indeed "for burning."[4] If comparative politics was not quite "sorcery,"[5] it certainly was plagued by a "new scholasticism."[6] As a result, a number of practitioners of the field began to drift toward safer havens: the more "empirical" area studies, the more abstract pursuit of methodologies or formal models, the more straightforward "normative theories," or the history of political ideas.

The institutional structure of the discipline, while not in itself the cause of the crisis, was one of the factors impeding its resolution. Nominally, the discipline was pluralistic and highly decentralized, with hundreds of departments and thousands of academic chairs competing with each other. But the appearance was deceptive. For underneath the surface of pluralism, the discipline was tightly controlled from a rather monolithic center, reflecting the circumstance that comparative politics came to this country as a matter of conscious choice and national priority. At the apex of this centralized structure were a dozen or so members of major departments who, by virtue of their prestige as well as of their overlapping memberships on the advisory boards of foundations, government agencies, journals, and university presses, acted as the principal arbiters of intellectual taste and set the standards for professional success. The problem was not the abuse of power, but intellectual inbreeding: a small group of people conducting intellectual dialogues among themselves, too easily persuaded that nondisciples were incompetent or not up to the intellectual standards required by truly scientific inquiry. Thus while in the traditional German, British—and indeed American—university systems, each major institution created its own "school," engaging in vigorous debate with all the others, in the postwar American academe there was to be only a single school of political sociology, based on the paradigm of modernization and development. Since America dominated the social sciences from 1945 to 1965, the paradigm crisis was in the first place an American crisis.

Contributing to the intellectual monopoly of neo-liberal political science was the decline, or dormancy, of its major competitors, the Marxists. There were several reasons for this temporary decline. One was the association of Marxist theory with Soviet Communism, now a totalitarian antagonist and a major international rival, which cast a pall of suspicion over its Western practitioners, however far they may have been removed from Stalinist practice. But there were other, perhaps still more potent, intellectual reasons for the lack of appeal of Marxist theory. In the first two postwar decades, social science was overwhelmed by the economic miracles of the Western industrial world, which made a shambles out of the most sacred Marxian tenets, such as the progressive immiseration of workers under conditions of capitalism. The Leninist theory of imperialism, with its emphasis on self-destructive competition among capitalists, was meanwhile discredited by the division of the world into deeply antagonistic socialist and capitalist camps. In the face of such evidence, Marxism hit the lowest ebb in its history. In the Communist East it was propped up by bayonets, but intellectually it was reduced to sterility. In the West, it was dismissed as nonsense and left for dead in the field, with some of its earlier practitioners having crossed over into the liberal, and still later into the conservative, camps of philosophy and social science.

The dominant position of neo-liberal social science and of the theory of modernization came to an abrupt end in the late 1960's under the impact of developments that shattered the complacent world of established social science. One of these developments was the rise of radical sentiment during the Vietnam era. This sentiment provided the handful of intellectual dissenters with a new audience, constituency, and power base, whence they could attack the "establishment," denouncing its social science as an ideology and a coercive instrument. As the rebellion unfolded in all of its raucousness, the "marginal men" of the recent past found readers and publishing outlets—mainly, one should note, through profit-oriented private enterprise, rather than the often stodgy subsidized presses. In due time, they also found academic appointments, through which their craft now became part of the "system."

None of this, however, would have happened without concurrent developments that resulted in the partial rehabilitation and resurrection of Marxism as an intellectual construct. In part, at least, this resurrection was the product of a revolution in the gathering of data as dozens of "new" nations were emerging from an age of statistical darkness. Mainly as a consequence of the work of international organizations, the world became aware of new facts—above all, the fact that, developmental efforts notwithstanding, disparities of income between rich and poor nations were increasing rather than declining. Whatever the reasons for this, at first sight the disparity seemed to provide new proof for the validity of old theories, especially the hallowed theory of immiseration, not within the modern nation-state, but within the larger international community. The stage was now set for a genuine paradigm shift.

Specifically, the intellectual breakthrough of these years involved two major innovations that together amounted to the formulation of a new paradigm. First, the focus of political inquiry shifted from the narrower Durkheimian concept of the division of labor within a society to the division of labor on a larger, global scale and, as a corollary, from the concept of social stratification to stratification among national societies, located in the core, periphery, and semiperiphery of a loosely structured world "system." In this new, spatially expanded universe, economic classes still remain the basic units of analysis. For though the international community consists of national states, these states are composed of classes; furthermore, the states themselves may be seen to behave like so many economic classes, competing with each other in an arena of scarcities and inequalities. So defined, the world becomes an arena of conflict that conventional theories of international relations tended to ignore or underestimate. Thus, whereas the older approaches emphasize the struggle for power among relatively equal sovereign entities, the new approach to international politics directs our attention to the struggle for scarce resources between rich and poor, or have and have-not, nations. In so doing, it gives us a new perspective on much of modern history, including the history of the two world wars, and still more broadly on the relations of great powers since the end of the eighteenth century.

Second, the intellectual innovations of recent years represent a breakthrough because they shed new light on the nature of interdependence in the modern world, contributing to our understanding of the nexus among processes in the core and the peripheries of the world economy. Even before this paradigmatic breakthrough, of course, there was some awareness of "linkages" between processes internal and external to the social system.[7] But in the new sociology these linkages have been endowed with a zero-sum quality, to borrow an expression from game theory. Thus the modernization of the core societies acquires global relevance, not only because—as Gerschenkron, Huntington, Black, and others well recognized—it triggers decisions to imitate it, but also because development in one sector of the world may cause decay in another. This zero-sum concept need not be construed to imply a mathematically precise inverse relationship. It merely implies that economic progress in one sector of the world economy may be the cause of political strain or decay in another.

This zero-sum concept of core-periphery relations is of key importance to the understanding of the new political sociology and economy. But precisely because of its centrality to the paradigm, it raises significant questions of causality, which students of the phenomenon have answered in a number of different ways. From these answers, then, there emerged three different theories, indeed, three different schools of thought, concerning the nature and dynamics of the modern world system. In the rest of this chapter we will examine these.

Neo-Marxism: Exploitation and Dependence

Although the new global perspective developed somewhat fitfully through the contributions of numerous social scientists of different ideological and methodological persuasions, its first and most obvious promoters have been Marxist scholars, most of them outsiders to the powerful academic establishment of the United States.[8] Passionate in their rejection of the status quo and firmly entrenched in their radical intellectual tradition, these proponents of the world-system approach found an explanation for the zero-sum nature of core-periphery relations in the classical concept of exploitation, or surplus transfer. In this mode of thinking, the development of the core economies is not only harmful to the welfare of the peripheries, but has been attained at their very expense, by reducing them to the status of dependencies and by successfully expropriating and transferring their surplus.[9] In André Gunder Frank's words,

economic development and underdevelopment are opposite faces of the same coin. . . . Both are the necessary result and contemporary manifestation of contradictions in the world capitalist system. . . . They are the product of a single, but dialectically contradictory economic structure and process [whereby] the metropolis expropriates economic surplus from its satellites and appropriates it for economic development.[10]

Or, in the still starker and terser formula of Harry Magdoff,

The higher standard of living and the greater amount of capital accumulated in Western Europe are rooted in past and present advantages, obtained by the latter through the exploitation of colonies and neo-colonial countries.[11]

This, however, is only the beginning. For although neo-Marxist scholars agree on the quintessentially expropriatory nature of the modern world system, they differ concerning the mechanics and modes of expropriation. A major dividing line here runs between the political and the economic theories of surplus transfer, reflecting Marx's own dichotomized way of thinking (or indecision) about this matter. Whereas the first theory relates the expropriation of surplus to the exercise of power by strong actors, the second puts the blame on the market mechanism, emphasizing, as Marx did, the preeminent role of labor in creating value and the unequal nature of the exchange relationship in labor markets.

Let us first examine political theories of expropriation as they derive from classical theories of imperialism. At their simplest, these theories assume that markets can function only when policed by powerful actors and suggest that the influence of the latter may supersede any presumed equilibrium between supply and demand. To put it more simply, leading powers in the international system are seen to have the ability to structure the terms of exchange to their own fundamental advantage. The most frequently cited example in proof of this point is the low price of energy in the decades following World War II, presumably related to the ability of the United States to dictate prices and to prevent the use of effective marketing strategies by politically weak producers. Other scenarios of expropriation point to more formal arrangements regulating the relationships between metropolitan and peripheral countries. These arrangements may entail direct or indirect forms of control over the behavior of primary producers. Thus, in some instances, the metropolitan nation may exercise day-to-day administrative influence over its satellites, in the manner of classical colonialism.[12] In others, the structure of control will include subservient "clientele classes"[13] or multinational corporations, whose nefarious activities have been chronicled in a vast body of literature that has come into being over the last fifteen years.[14] The idiom used throughout this literature is that of the political Left, but it bears more than superficial resemblance to an earlier body of political writings generated by the European Right. That literature, too, used the idiom of expropriation, but instead of the multinationals it excoriated the Rothschilds and Jewish finance capital for having no fatherland, for being elusive and conspiratorial, and for being deleterious to the interests of the weaker nation states of the European periphery.

What then about economic theories of exploitation? They too have several variants. In one, associated with the names of André Gunder Frank, Theotonio Dos Santos, and James O'Connor, the transfer of surplus is the result of trade.[15] The inspiration for this theory comes straight from classical Marxism. Just as Marx does in *Capital* and elsewhere,[16] these writers adhere to the view that the ultimate measure of value is labor time, and they distinguish between "lower" and "higher" ranking goods. The former are essentials that require large amounts of "direct" labor to produce; the latter require small amounts of labor time given the high degree of mechanization in the production process. Typically, according to these writers, the countries of the periphery produce lower ranking goods and exchange them for the higher ranking goods produced in the core countries. When this happens, value is being transferred from one economic sector to another. By working larger amounts of time for one unit of exchange, the labor force of the periphery in effect subsidizes the labor force of the core countries. It permits the core entrepreneurs to pay higher wages *and* to reap higher profits at the same time. Thus in the long run conditions in the core economies improve, while economies of the peripheries deteriorate. The logic seems to be impeccable. And if the fundamental premise of the theory is correct, Frank and his disciples have created an intellectually forceful explanation for growing regional income disparities in the modern world. In the process they have also managed to rescue the classical theory of relative immiseration within the larger context of the global economy.

Though this theory has been touted as one of the marketplace, like its Marxist forerunner, it is not a purely economic theory. It does argue, as we have seen, that different levels of labor productivity among trading partners result in the transfer of value from one to another. It also points to the progressive capitalization of value within the economy of the stronger trading partner: the labor of the peripheral worker is transformed into labor-saving machinery in the metropolitan system of production. But what is the explanation for the initial disparity that starts the cycle of exploitation and reinvestment of the expropriated surplus? The answer here is bluntly political. For whereas liberal economists would be disposed to point out the economic value of innovation and ingenuity, the Marxist theory of primitive accumulation refers us to the violent misdeeds of early capitalism. The capitalist system of exchange may well function as an impersonal mechanism free from the volition of individual actors. But the roots of the system are to be found in the vice of warfare and not in the virtues of innovative behavior. So formulated, the theory of unequal exchange, like the labor theory of value, acquires a strong ethical, if not a downright theological, component, which makes it eminently suitable as a political instrument.

Perhaps the single most ambitious work to take advantage of this neo-Marxist concept of surplus transfer is Immanuel Wallerstein's opus on the origins of the capitalist world economy, *The Modern World System*. Designed to put the problem of international income inequality into historical perspective by surveying a vast array of Marxist as well as neo-Marxist writings, Wallerstein's study is a model of painstaking research, full of intriguing insights concerning relationships between economics and politics. Like Frank, Wallerstein accepts the distinction between higher and lower ranking goods, defining the latter as "goods whose labor is less well rewarded, but which [are] an integral part of the overall system of the division of labor, because the commodities involved are essential for daily use."[17] He also accepts the notion that in the exchange of these goods value is transferred from one trading partner to another. But his way of conceptualizing coercion in the modern world system seems to deviate from that of other neo-Marxist writers—for which he has been roundly criticized by some as a "neo-Smithian" theorist.[18] For Wallerstein coercion is latent in state-to-state relationships but is overt in the periphery, where the elites exercise and institutionalize it in order to extract surplus from their own populations and thereby to import luxuries. Therefore, the rise of the modern world system has not only resulted in a new global division of labor between the producers of higher and lower ranking goods. It has also been accompanied by a growing polarity between two types of social and political organization. For while societies of the core evolved a system of free wage labor, those of the periphery have adopted increasingly repressive forms of labor organization. Thus, from Wallerstein's point of view, elites of peripheral societies are not puppets and clients but independent actors, although "objectively" their behavior in the long run serves the interests of the core elites. For by trading with the core societies on unequal terms, the peripheral ruling class contributes to regional income disparity and undermines its own political position in the international system.

Whatever the validity of his argument, Wallerstein is very effective in portraying the economic and political differentiation of the "European world system" after the sixteenth century. Indeed, his portrayal of facts is both forceful and consonant with the views of most historians. Few today would argue the point that while the Occident was moving away from servile labor, the countries of Eastern Europe and Latin America were moving in the opposite direction of "neo-serfdom," reinstating servile labor under the guise of legal emancipation and economic equality.

But Wallerstein is less successful, and certainly more ambivalent, in dealing with the pivotal question of his work concerning the origins of the modern world system. On the one hand, his book contains an elaborate—perhaps overly elaborate— discussion of the rise of the European state system and identifies the state as the principal agent of capitalist economic development. For Wallerstein modern states function to guarantee profits: they shift the loss of enterprise to society as a whole, while making sure that "economic gain is distributed to private hands."[19] In this vein Wallerstein argues the case comparing England and Spain: "It was not . . . that Spain was somehow less entrepreneurial than other parts of Europe," but that "Spain did not erect (probably because she could not erect) the kind of state machinery which would enable the dominant classes of Spain to profit from the creation of a European world-economy."[20] And yet, in contrast to Marx's *Capital*, organized force is described both as a cause and a consequence of economic change.[21] An economy grows because the state is strong, but states also become strong as a result of economic development. The reasoning here is circular, and to break out of it Wallerstein suggests that, in the last analysis, the rise of the modern core was a matter of historical accident. In the late middle ages "either Eastern Europe would become the 'breadbasket' of Western Europe, or vice versa." In the given "conjuncture . . . either solution would have served the 'needs of the situation.' A *slight* edge determined which of the two alternatives would prevail. At which point, the *slight* edge of the fifteenth century became the great disparity of the seventeenth, and the monumental difference of the nineteenth."[22]

However, differences in the organic composition of capital—the ratio between costs of labor and machinery—represent only one possible starting point for theorizing about the transfer of advantage by trading, and neo-Marxist scholarship has developed a number of alternative approaches. A case in point is Arghiri Emmanuel's theory of unequal exchange.[23] In the face of empirical objections by some of its critics,[24] this theory holds that the critical components of core-periphery trade are not primary, but processed goods and further, that labor productivity in the core and in the critical export sectors of peripheral economies varies only to an insignificant degree. According to Emmanuel, what is different in the two sectors is not the organic composition of capital, the ratio between labor and machinery, but the wages paid to the workers. For the same amount and kind of labor, workers of the core and periphery are remunerated at different rates. This is possible for one of two reasons. Either authoritarian state machines prevent the effective unionization of the labor force in the industrial sector, or a labor-repressive local agriculture provides cheap comestibles to the urban workers. In either case, non-economic coercion is seen to loom large in the societies of the periphery, an observation with which it is not difficult to agree. But the question is who benefits? Is it the elite of the peripheral society or the consuming public of the core region? Emmanuel's theory of the "imperialism of trade" suggests that it is the latter and that the oppressed and ill-paid workers of the backward societies subsidize the standard of living in the advanced industrial world. A worker in Detroit or Düsseldorf enjoys a high standard of living because someone somewhere in Brazil, Taiwan, or the Philippines produces sweaters and trench coats at wages close to the subsistence level. Remarkably, in the light of recent economic experience, the theory does not contemplate the potential ill-effects of these exports on the economic prosperity and employment of factory workers in the industrial countries.

If in the best Marxist tradition Frank, Wallerstein, and Emmanuel emphasize the production of goods and the labor time involved in the production of commodities, some theories on the borderlines of Marxism have shifted their attention to the service sector. From this new twist on the labor theory of value, the notion of a "dual labor market" has emerged in political economy.[25] According to this notion, in the global core capitalists are forced to compete for the highly trained and skilled labor required to utilize complex technologies. Here, the classical principles of the market apply, and the labor theory of value is not directly operative. However, another and highly imperfect market mechanism operates on the periphery, where members of a large reserve army of the unemployed are vying for employment in a largely low-skill service sector, forced to sell their labor power in exchange for subsistence wages. In this manner they provide cheap amenities to the workers of the core, thus contributing directly both to the rising rate of profit and to social peace in the advanced industrial countries. For proof we are referred to the amenities provided by workers in the tourist industries of less developed countries, to guest workers occupying low-paid service jobs, or to migrant labor in the agricultural sector of the core economies.

Finally, under the general heading of surplus transfer, we have to take note of theories that set out to explain the potential disadvantages of peripheral societies in terms of variations in the income elasticities of demand for primary and secondary products. The heart of the argument, popularized by Raul Prebisch and his associates, is that as per capita income increases in industrial nations, their consumers will spend progressively smaller shares of their income on comestibles and primary products. The opposite appears to be the case in the poor countries of the periphery, where imports of manufactured goods tend to be out of proportion to the level of national income. This produces a steady deterioration in the terms of trade.[26] The argument was originally derived from the experience of several tropical trading countries and seems to have been fully borne out by their experience. When extended from this narrower context to the experience of Latin America as a whole or when advanced as a full-fledged theory of international income inequality, however, the validity of the construct becomes more problematic. The issue is complicated by the fact that many Third World countries are not exporters of comestibles but of energy and raw materials, and in this broader context the argument concerning the income elasticity of demand is of a limited relevance. Americans may spend progressively smaller amounts of their income on bananas but not on oil or copper. And if the imports of some primary goods have declined, as in the case of raw silk or cotton, this has had less to do with demand than with technological innovations, specifically with the invention of synthetic fibers and of other substitutes for raw products. But whatever its empirical validity, in its pure form the argument is neither inherently Marxist nor radical. It becomes radical only within the context of certain assumptions that attribute the excessive consumption of core manufactured goods to manipulative and seductive core behavior or to collusion between the upper-class consumers of the periphery and the elites of the core.

Beyond Surplus Transfer: Anderson and Skocpol

To put these theories in perspective, let us reiterate that, by taking the critical step from the social to the global system, they have broadened the scope of political discourse and set up the discipline for a new synthesis. But as we noted in the beginning of this essay, a paradigm is not yet theory, and the neo-Marxist attempt to transform paradigm into theory has raised a good number of questions. Some of these are as old as Marxist theory itself. To begin with, is the labor theory of value really a theory? Or is it merely an ethical-normative statement to the effect that certain types of economic behavior, above all risk-taking entrepreneurship, should not be rewarded, on the ground that under ideal conditions—that is, socialism—they can be dispensed with? And further, can these types of behavior, together with the genius of the inventor-innovator, be reduced to labor time or to the costs of producing and reproducing the inventor's labor power? Finally, can one assume, as Marxists do, that ingenuity and creativity are relatively abundant qualities, relatively evenly distributed among societies, thus rendering any concept of cultural differences irrelevant? Clearly, the validity of theories of unequal exchange and surplus transfer depends on affirmative answers to these questions.

If the problems of the economic theories of exploitation are conceptual, those of the political theories are empirical and quantitative in character. To put it differently, one need not be a Marxist scholar to recognize the role of force in international relations and the fact that all too often in history force, or the threat of force, has been used to transfer resources and advantages from one group of states to another. As Thucydides reminds us, the powerful exact what they can, and the weak surrender what they must. Modern history has not rendered this piece of wisdom irrelevant. But the question remains whether such acts of force and exploitation, however frequent, are in and of themselves sufficient to account for the whole pattern of regional income disparities in the modern world. Unfortunately, it is not easy to answer this question conclusively. To try to answer it with a string of horror stories is tempting but not very useful. At the same time, the attempt to draw up neat balance sheets of costs and benefits over the span of centuries is not particularly feasible, and its results can always be challenged on the ground that an amount, however small, may have provided the critical edge at a particular historical juncture. Thus, before we are ready to close the books on exploitation, we may be well advised to consider a few alternative hypotheses.

One of these alternative hypotheses emerges from the works of Perry Anderson and Theda Skocpol, both of whom try to avoid the pitfalls of the labor theory of value by shifting the burden of explanation from the global economy to the international political arena of competing national states.[27] This is not to say that either of these authors is impervious to the importance of economic factors. On the contrary, both Anderson, who is a professed Marxist, and Skocpol, who is not, recognize that the postmedieval ascendancy of the Occident in the international political system was closely related to successful economic development capable of sustaining armies and navies on a hitherto unimaginable scale. Though not clearly stated, the heart of the argument appears to be that once this occidental ascendancy had been attained, it put competitive pressures on the rest of the political entities of the world to create and maintain modern armies despite the relative backwardness of their economies. The problem of these backward competitors had been that although the productive potential of national societies is highly unequal, the unit cost of international military power is relatively equal. Given this imbalance, the same level of military preparedness requires progressively larger proportions of national income as we move from the global core to the peripheries. In turn, the greater the imbalance, the greater the pressure on the state to turn itself into a coercive instrument for extracting the resources needed for effective competition. These "accelerating pressures"[28] and relative scarcities then explain the different lineages of western, central, and eastern European absolutism (Anderson); the incidence of popular revolutions in countries like France, Russia, and China that have also been major actors in world politics; and finally, the rise of "centralized, bureaucratic, mass incorporative states with enhanced great power potential"[29] in the first half of the twentieth century.

Neither Anderson nor Skocpol uses elaborate statistics to bolster their points. But both the admittedly scarce historical materials and the somewhat more ample contemporary ones seem to lend credence to their arguments. Thus we find that the expenditures of peripheral states (including their defense component) have, since the middle of the nineteenth century, tended to represent a greater percentage of national income than do such expenses in advanced industrial countries, though the pattern is sometimes disrupted by the collapse of some governments under the burden of overspending.[30] We also find a few notable exceptions, among them prerevolutionary Russia and China. But these exceptions only tend to corroborate further Skocpol's point, for after their successful revolutions both countries reentered the world arena as relatively profligate defense spenders. Indeed, nothing is more illustrative of the validity of the central argument than a comparison of contemporary Soviet and American defense spending. While the preparedness of these two countries is generally assumed to be on a par, this parity eats up more than twice as much of Soviet as of American national income. Whatever the original aims of the great Bolshevik revolution, its most important result has been to create an extractive state, with a vastly "enhanced great power potential."

While the role of the state is central to their theoretical concerns, both Anderson and Skocpol pay considerable attention to social structures, especially to institutional arrangements in the agricultural sector of the economy with which a particular society is "entering" the competitive modern international system. These two factors, the social and the global, do not appear separately. Rather, they are interrelated elements of the same analytic scheme. Whereas the qualities of the world system explain the pressures that a peripheral state will inevitably have to face, configurations in the social system explain how effectively, and in what manner, these pressures will be met. By paying attention to both, Skocpol and Anderson introduce a kind of balance into their analysis that is absent from both the conventional theories of development and the mainline theories of dependence.

Dependence: Structural or Psychological?

Valid as this argument may be, like the various arguments of exploitation, it tells us only part of the story of core-periphery relations. In order to round out this story, we must turn to yet another theory, based on the concepts of relative deprivation and the international demonstration effect, or IDE. The elements of this theory, scattered in the works of a number of economists, sociologists, and political scientists, do not per se invalidate alternative explanations for the "development of underdevelopment."[31] Rather, they supersede these explanations by pointing to sources of tension in the modern world that are far more general than either the phenomenon of expropriation or the pressures for military spending.

Central to this theory is the notion that the material standards, life-styles, and expectations of the urban-industrial civilization of the Occident exert a powerful psychological appeal and that given this appeal, these styles and expectations are diffused faster than the technological and institutional innovations required to sustain them, thus creating imbalances between aspirations and reality. Over time, these imbalances will produce declining rates of saving, or if savings are extracted by force, they will create a sense of relative deprivation and therefore the potential for social conflict. Moreover, since the use of force itself requires effort and the expenditure of resources, the prospects of development are likely to suffer either way. In a seemingly circular fashion, underdevelopment at Time 1 becomes the cause of more underdevelopment at Time 2. To put it differently, the progress of the world system has its own dialectic, in which solutions (abundance) in one sector produce problems (scarcity) in another, and in the long run bring about crises in the larger entity.

The terms "demonstration effect" and "relative deprivation" are of fairly recent vintage, but the ideas underlying them are not inventions of our own day. Thus, about a hundred years ago, in one of his lesser-known essays, Max Weber examined the impoverishment of the Prussian *Junkers* and linked it to the spread of the urban life styles of the new bourgeois class in the western provinces of Germany and in the western countries of the Continent.[32] Marx was likewise well aware of the relativity of poverty and riches. This, at least, is the inference we can draw from his theory of relative immiseration and from his observation that the rise of a palace turns the house next door into a hut.[33] But neither Marx nor Weber built on their insights, and in the end it was not they but Veblen who addressed the problem systematically by formulating the psychological and cultural theory of consumption that Marxism lacks.

According to Veblen, one of the basic rules of economic life is that new products are first acquired by elites. But thereafter consumption patterns "spread with great facility through the body of population by the force of emulative imitation,"[34] in part because prior acquisition by the elite puts the stamp of status upon them. In the modern period, however, the diffusion of consumer styles accelerates because, by their very nature, the products of the scientific and technological revolutions are desirable not only for social but also for profoundly human reasons. The innovations of the modern world affect not only status but also the quality, indeed the very quantity, or duration, of precious human life. Hence, Veblen tells us, they create "standards of reputable expenditure, also called 'decent living,' and a lesion suffered in falling short of such standard of 'decent living' is of spiritual nature. [For this reason] as among the indigent, so among the wealthy, this standardized scale of expenditures will come to be mandatory . . . and accepted as a staple of decency."[35] In this manner "usages, standards and prejudices . . . no less exacting than the conventions which govern industry and business"[36] will make their way downward from one class to another. Veblen does not say so, but by analogy one can extend these observations from the upper and lower classes to the rich and poor nations of the world. If we do so, the "standards of reputable expenditure" turn into an international demonstration effect.

Although most contemporary writers are inclined to use these Veblenian insights to explain the current plight of Third World countries, the concept is also eminently applicable to the historical experience of the European peripheries. Indeed, it is here in the backyard of the Occident that we can best observe the potentially deleterious consequences of Western progress, examine the relationship between innovation and expectations, and subject the theory of the IDE to an empirical test. The innovations here refer to the great economic revolutions of the postmedieval world and in particular to the revolutions in agricultural and industrial production, whose intersection in time seems to have set the pattern for the economic differentiation of the European continent.

The first of these historic innovations was revolutionary in name only, for in reality it refers to piecemeal changes in the methods of agricultural production in Northwest Europe and to the painfully slow diffusion of these innovations toward the South and the East of the Continent. Overall, it seems that it took no less than 200 years for crop yields to double in the core area of innovation—Flanders, the Rhineland, and southern England—and that the improved methods of plowing, fertilizing, and crop rotation spread at a snail-like pace of three to four miles per year across the adjacent continental landmass. At this rate the technologies that had been modern in Holland around 1600 reached Hungary, Poland, and the southern tip of the Iberian peninsula at about the year 1800, the Balkans and Russia still later. However, since innovation in the northwest "triangle" was not a one-time affair but an ongoing process, regions located 600 to 800 miles from the epicenter of innovation were still some 200 years behind the core region in terms of per acre yields and labor productivity. In other words, the distribution of income on the Continent had acquired a neatly regressive geographical pattern, with core, peripheral, and semiperipheral regions all clearly discernible in terms of per capita product and the structure of the agricultural economy.

The second revolution, with its roots in England, is more appropriately designated as such, for it produced a truly dramatic upswing in both production and consumption. Between 1780 and 1830, industrial production in England increased about 20-fold, led by a 33-fold increase in the production of textiles over a 36-year period.[37] Growth in the volume of production resulted in an overall decline in industrial prices, in changing consumption patterns, and in the rapid redefinition of what Veblen referred to as the "standards of reputable expenditure." The luxuries of years past—articles of hygiene, body linen, seasonal fashions, household furniture—became articles of common consumption, if not for all classes, then for a sufficiently large number of people who henceforth could regard themselves as a genuine middle class, positioned between the desperately poor and the conspicuously consuming rich.

That these standards spread rapidly from the innovative core to the imitative peripheries is well recorded in both social history and in fiction. Indeed, by the middle of the nineteenth century, all over the European continent and in many other parts of the world, the urban, the middle, and the educated classes had accepted the life-style of their Western counterparts: they had discovered seasonal fashions, taken to the wearing of Western garb, traveled to occidental countries, and acquired artifacts produced in the great manufacturing centers of the core as a matter of "civilization." As one observer of Romania noted in 1828, "perfumes, champagne, glass, silverware, mirrors, matches, furniture spread rapidly among the members of the upper and middle classes."[38] Or, to quote a

Hungarian writer of the same decade: "People are developing new tastes all the time. Silverware, so far only seen in the houses of the rich, now make their appearance in many households. The watch, once as rare as a white crow, has now turned into an article of necessity."[39] In the Balkans "tea, coffee, sugar were passing out of the class of luxury goods into common use. Better-off households bought some furniture and household utensils. . . . Town-made lamps were replacing home-made candles."[40] In Latin America, meanwhile, the historian records a "breathless desire to be like the French and the British . . . to dress like fashionable Europeans," so that people "went about building their houses, educating their young, and spending their leisure time"[41] like the denizens of industrial countries. "The houses of the better classes were [thus] as replete with objects of English and American manufacture as would be true for the citizen of London or Boston."[42] Trade statistics tend to bear out these impressions, with the soaring imports reflecting the fateful fact that these consumption patterns were being grafted upon economies that were ill equipped to sustain them.[43]

Obviously, the less developed an economy was, the greater would be the gap between expectation and reality, and the greater the pressures for disinvestment and debt spending. Unwittingly, therefore, the industrial revolution of England created not only new styles of life but also economic and social imbalances that in most cases not even massive state intervention could remedy. Indeed, in the case of Europe, we will find today the same geographically neat, regressive pattern of income distribution that was bequeathed upon the Continent by the preindustrial age. This pattern transcends political and ethnic boundaries and does not correlate with either power or volumes of trade; hence it cannot be readily accounted for either by exploitation or by conventional theories of culture and national character.

However, the study of the IDE in a historical context provides us not only with new explanations for the "development of underdevelopment" but also presents us with new insights into the dynamics of class formation on the peripheries of the modern world economy. In this respect, three processes of change stand out. The first of these is the decline of the middle strata of peripheral societies, the traditional merchant and artisan classes, and the lesser producers among the agrarian gentry, whose plight is the staple of nineteenth-century novels from Russia to the Iberian peninsula. The story of these classes, whether the *knezina* chiefs of Serbia, the *chorbadjii* of Bulgaria, the *dzsentri* of Hungary, the small *boyars* of Romania, the *Krautjunkers* of Prussia, or the *patriciates minores* of Latin America,[44] seem to follow closely the same pattern: it leads from a brief flurry of commercial activity to gradual discouragement, indebtedness, and retreat from entrepreneurship, and finally escape from economic activity to education to become, in the graphic phrase of one East European writer, a "proletariat of the pen."[45] Less graphically, the terms "intelligentsia," and more recently, "new middle class"[46] refer to the results of the very same process.

Historically, this decline of the "traditional," or "pre-entry" middle classes was accompanied by a second phenomenon indirectly related to the IDE—the rise of immigrant, ethnic, or other forms of "pariah entrepreneurship,"[47] to fill in the void left by the native element. The best known examples of this pattern of mobility are Jewish, Greek, Armenian, and Tsintsar entrepreneurship in Eastern Europe; Chinese and East European entrepreneurship in Southeast Asia and East Africa; and the role played by assorted immigrant groups on the Latin American continent. The key to understanding this phenomenon is neither culture nor luxury spending, but the Veblenian notion of status consumption. For as native-born elites hold on to their established status by adapting themselves to globalized standards of "decent living" and to ways "befitting a gentleman," they lost their ability to save and to accumulate. Their economic functions then are assumed by those who are not burdened by established norms and status expectations.

To round out this picture of social mobility, we must turn to the upper classes, the plantation owners and latifundiary aristocrats of the peripheral countries. Unlike the lesser gentry, these classes had shown considerable staying power throughout the nineteenth century and often beyond, if only because the vastness of their holdings permitted them to maintain themselves as status consumers even in the modern world. But modern consumption patterns, including travel to foreign countries, cut deep into their margins of saving and hence into their capacity to invest in modern production technologies. To compensate, country by country these latifundiary aristocracies emerged as powerful lobbies for a variety of labor-repressive measures. The all-too-familiar "retraditionalization" of these large producers and their role in restoring various forms of "second-serfdom," or "neo-serfdom"[48]—often after a brief spell of export-oriented economic and political liberalism—must thus be regarded as part and parcel of an overall socio-economic pattern that was the reverse side of Western material progress.

Still more significantly from our perspective, the IDE contributes to our understanding of the dynamics of "state building" on the peripheries of the modern industrial world. Historically, much as in present-day "emerging nations," these dynamics have been intimately related to status consumption, market pressures, and the desire of the declining, bankrupt native middle classes to maintain their status and relative income levels in the face of great changes in the core countries. As these classes were threatened by economic extinction and social decline, they attempted to save themselves by capturing the levers of power, by turning themselves into political classes, living off the institutions of the modern state. Thus, whereas the history of the Western state may well be described as one of the rising middle classes in quest for larger, national markets, the history of the peripheral states is one of declining middle classes, trying to escape from the market and to secure their social position by political, rather than economic, entrepreneurship.

In some instances, the native middle classes may become bureaucrats and military men in the service of a colonial power. But still more frequently, as in East Europe and in most of Latin America, they will place themselves in the forefront of movements of national independence, eager to possess a sovereign state of their own. Then, as they enter public service, they will quickly transform themselves into a "state bourgeoisie" and turn the state into a revenue-raising instrument, so as to secure for themselves standards set by the upper and middle classes of the advanced industrial societies. If and where this "state bourgeoisie" is efficient enough, it creates the proper legal instruments to generate incomes appropriate for a ruling elite. But if revenues cannot be raised in an orderly fashion, the public employees of the backward society will extort their share anyway, by "corruption" and semi-legal means. In either case, there will be income transfer, not from the periphery to the core, as Marxist scholarship stipulates, but from the lower to the middle and upper strata of the peripheral society itself. In this manner, the peripheral state will act as a grand equalizer, not among the different strata of its own citizenry, but between the local elite and the elites of advanced industrial states. Some inequality, to be sure, will remain between elite and elite. But these differences will be far less conspicuous than the income disparities between the labor force of the core countries and the underemployed masses of the periphery.

These historical patterns may well serve as a general model of politics and social mobility on the world peripheries, except that in the twentieth century we must add a new dimension to the politics of backwardness: the rise of mass dissatisfaction as a political factor, often referred to as the "entry of the masses" into national politics. This phenomenon, familiar to contemporary political science, has most frequently been explained by the "mobilizing" effects of development and social change, but especially by the spread of mass education and inclusion into global economic networks that expose the average person to Western influences as readily as the members of the elite.[49] This may well be an important insight. But in order to fully appreciate the phenomenon of mass politics, we also need to look at the other side of the coin, represented by developments external to the social system. Most significantly, we must look at the continued progress of the core economies, above all, at their historical change from middle-class to mass-consumption societies, whereby the lower classes began to acquire many of the amenities hitherto available only to the "privileged." This historical trend began to unfold during the first decades of this century. It slowed down somewhat during the interwar period and reached full maturity after World War II, when the societies of the West achieved material standards that few societies of the periphery could reasonably hope to emulate. Henceforth, peripheral states must respond not only to the consumer expectations of elites but also to those emanating from the lower classes. In a marketplace of great scarcities, these demands only further jeopardize the prospects of development policies and confront the peripheral society with the stark choice between the endemic crisis of "praetorianism," and the stark social and political discipline of "totalitarianism."

The "entry" of the masses into politics is closely intertwined with another aspect of class formation and modern politics, the rise of a "radical intelligentsia," characteristic of the societies of the periphery. Conventional explanations for the phenomenon are usually cast in terms of economic scarcity: too many people chasing too few jobs, with the losers in this race for mobility turning against the established order in bitter disappointment. The fact that in some instances—most notably in the case of the Russian *raznochinstvo*—members of this intelligentsia have been drawn from outside the traditional establishment tends to lend credence to this purely economic explanation. But a closer scrutiny of the evidence will lead us to alternative hypotheses. If we examine statistics pertaining to the school system in peripheral societies earlier in the century, we will be struck by the truly minute size of the educated public.[50] These small numbers could easily have been absorbed by the political establishments.

The quantitative argument becomes still more suspect if we consider that many of the radicals came from relatively comfortable backgrounds that could well have served as convenient stepping stones toward promising public careers. Surely, the Ulyanov brothers, young Bronstein-Trotsky, or George Lukács could easily have found a niche for themselves within the existing order. They certainly could have passed civil service exams or gone on to profitable careers in their fathers' businesses. That they did not do so was not from lack of opportunity but from the availability of the alternative, more risky, but ultimately more profitable, opportunity to become the leaders of deeply dissatisfied mass constituencies. Indeed, these people were not so much an "intelligentsia," meaning an educated public, as another political class, recruited from the most willing and able risk-takers in the talent pool of their societies. These entrepreneurial qualities, much more than formal education or the skill to manipulate symbols, distinguish these new political men (and women) from the dull and bureaucratized political establishments and explain their spectacular successes in the great revolutions of this century.

From these experiences, then, the IDE emerges as a ubiquitous source of relative scarcities and as a major force in shaping the structure of state and society on the global periphery. Our historical generalizations seem to be amply corroborated by studies of "imitative" and "status" consumption in the contemporary world.[51] Their validity is also borne out by the impressions of travelers to dozens of countries as diverse as Thailand, Argentina, Nigeria, or Poland, where either Western styles of consumption are conspicuously imitated by the

middle classes or their absence is just as conspicuously re-
sented. Perhaps still more persuasively, the political relevance
of the IDE is evident from the nervous reactions of the multitude of national radical, Communist, and religious funda-
mentalist regimes to what they habitually decry as the "cultural imperialism" of the West, and the "false needs," or
"materialism," generated by it.

There exist, to be sure, a number of studies that have attempted to marshal contrary evidence, in order to impeach
the validity of the hypothesis.[52] Still, even critics acknowledge
that the peoples, or at least the middle classes, of the non-
Western world today show conspicuous concern for their economic future,[53] or that "the demonstration effect of other peoples' material or political culture"[54] becomes socially relevant
in one form or another. Thus while Anthony Oberschall draws
attention to differences between desires and expectations,[55] his
research data show that in one African country 69 percent of
the respondents to a survey were dissatisfied with their own
material conditions and another 58 percent "did not own a
car, want[ed] it, but [did] not expect to get it."[56] (Percentages
for "electric light," and a "dark suit," were 50 and 37 respectively.[57]) The same study concludes that "Nigerians aspire . . .
not for some utopian or unattainable Western standard of
life," but merely for a "decent" standard that includes "a house
of their own," as well as such simple consumer goods and services as bicycles, radios, printed fabric for clothes, soft drinks
and bottled beer, schooling for their children, a clean water
supply, hospital and dispensaries.[58] Yet all of these *are* "Western," and inability to attain them *may* turn into frustration with
the existing state of affairs.

There is, of course, considerable merit to the argument
that exposure to the "material culture" of the West does not
lead "promptly" to aspirations "for new goods and ways of
life."[59] There is still more justification for the proposition that
the IDE becomes salient only under specific conditions and
that we should identify these before we can speak of a genuine

theory.[60] Most convincing here is the proposition that relative
scarcities become salient only when there is change in the beliefs "that justify increased or different expectations,"[61] when
old beliefs collapse or when some new doctrine tells people
that they are "in the same boat" with their more prosperous
brethren. This stands to reason and is borne out by historical
experience. Thus the great revolutionary movements of the
periphery—of which more will be said in Chapter 4—did not
arise just because international income inequalities had passed
a particular threshold but also because progressive increases
in the international income gap coincided with major events—
the world wars and the great commodity crises of the past century—that shattered universal belief in progress and in the
Western conception of civilization, which had provided ideological underpinnings to the nineteenth-century liberal world
system.

FOUR

Communism and Revolution

Communism: A Global Strategy

Having examined the historical experiences of the peripheries, we may go back a few steps in time to compare them with those of the core countries. If we do so, we can construct two distinct models of politics and political change. In the first, enshrined in the categories of classical theory, politics implies the management of social change, and political change is a response to the social consequences of technological innovation. The second model emerges from the experience of the peripheral countries and is summarized in the various conceptions of a modern world system. In it, politics means the management of international inequalities and the tensions arising from the condition of backwardness. Political change here predates technological innovation and social change in one's own society.

The question is, then, how political elites may go about managing the tensions of backwardness and international inequality. One typical way of addressing the problem is by adopting a strategy of "development." This strategy, as neoclassical theorists will tell us, implies a systematic attempt on the part of the elites of a backward society—and possibly of their allies in the advanced societies of the world—to "reduce their 'atimic' [meaning here, apparently, outdated] status," and to catch up with "other, well-placed nations."[1] Such an endeavor requires marshaling one's own resources, borrowing the latest technologies, and experimenting with new social and political institutions congruent with the new system of production and distribution. The term "modernization" is equally appropriate here. For just as one modernizes one's electric kitchen by acquiring the latest and presumably most efficient gadgetry, so the backward nation modernizes its economy and society by acquiring "state of the art" technologies and the know-how to operate them.

Although the idea of "catching up" with the "well-placed" nations goes back to the early modern age, it was only in the nineteenth century that it matured into a coherent political strategy to which we can apply the neo-liberal label. This strategy was "neo" in comparison with the economic and political practices of older European states, above all those of England, because it was ready to subordinate domestic markets to the state by regulating wages and prices and the flow of investment from the centers of political power. Yet while engaging in protectionism, labor repression, and, on occasion, entrepreneurship, these developmental states remained true to the original liberal model in two significant ways. First, they entered the world market as willing players, never challenging its utility and legitimacy as a distributive mechanism of the last resort. Second, under the moral influence of the West, these states were ready to accept significant legal and institutional restraints on their domestic and international behavior and, by implication, on the pursuit of their developmental objectives. This did not necessarily result in working parliamentary institutions based on the British model. But most peripheral nations of the time were ready to accept the restraints of law and international public opinion and to curb the worst forms of excess toward their neighbors and their own subjects. The abandonment of arbitrary government, the introduction of a Western-style judicial process, and respect for international law became conditions for acceptance into a "civilized" community of nations, as defined by the leading countries of the Occident. Failure to abide by these standards was construed as a sign of cultural incompetence and political immaturity, to be rectified in extreme cases by foreign intervention and colonial rule.

The universality and legitimacy of these principles began to erode around the turn of the century, heralding a number of significant changes in the political management of international inequalities. The reasons for this erosion were numerous, and not all of them can easily be accommodated within a theory of scarcity. True, at least in part, these changes were related to the gulf between rich and poor nations, which not only persisted but increased, despite considerable effort on the part of the latter to close it. But to a large extent these changes were also due to the gradual erosion of the "charisma," or mystique, of the Occident and to a decline of its moral authority in the wake of a number of devastating economic crises, such as the "great commodity crisis" of 1878–96 and especially World War I, the horrors of which did much to destroy the Spencerian liberal myth that advanced societies were also societies of peace and superior virtue.

These historical developments gave rise to the first "national radical" movements on the peripheries. These movements inherited from the past the liberal commitment to nationalism and a view of the world consisting of competing national states. Yet at the same time they rejected the liberal notion of restraint. Indeed, they charged that the legal state and parliamentary government were only so many ruses, invented and imposed by the core nations to impede the already disadvantaged peripheries in their attempt to compete effectively with the privileged nations of the earth. The new slogan became *sacro egoismo*, exhorting nations to emancipate themselves from the shackles of law in both their domestic and international affairs, so as to be able to pursue their happiness by any means. To some of the lesser nations of the world, in Eastern Europe and Latin America, this meant that governments should pursue developmental goals by radical techniques of mobilization. To some of the larger, more aggressive nations, like Fascist Italy, it meant that heroic-military exploits and plunder could now replace economic competition in free markets as a means of winning the "proletarian nations" of the world a "place under the sun" of privilege.

However, the same historical period produced a range of strategies to solve the problem of international inequality. These strategies proposed to change the human condition, not by the transfer of technologies or by tinkering with the social structure of particular societies, but by changing the very structure and operational principles of the larger world system. A few of these movements—above all, the democratic socialists, or Social Democrats—accepted the liberal idea of moral and legal restraints on the power of states. But the great radical, or "totalitarian," movements of this century—the communists, populists, and the national (or more accurately racial) socialists—had as little to say about modernization as they had about law or morality in the pursuit of their ultimate historical objectives. True, their respective images of the future varied as much as the choice of their particular means, and it is in terms of these variations that we can distinguish between radical movements of the Left and the Right. Communism and populism were, at least in their pristine forms, movements of the Left. For although their views on technology and science differed substantially, they both set out to create a world of fundamental equality beyond the market, to be attained by revolution, that is, by mobilizing mass discontent. National socialism, meanwhile, was a movement of the Right in that it pursued the vision of a world of inequality, hierarchy, and command, to be attained by mobilizing the military potential of a few national or racial communities. These differing political movements and systems are summarized schematically in Table 2 and Table 3.

Of these three movements populism never got off the

TABLE 2
Political Movements and Systems

| | | FUNDAMENTAL PRINCIPLE | |
		Restraint	No restraint
FUNDAMENTAL PURPOSE	Development	Liberalism Neo-liberalism	Radical nationalism
	New global system	Social democracy	Populism Communism National (racial) socialism

TABLE 3
Globalist Radical Movements

| | | ENDS | | |
| | | Equality | | |
		Industrial	Rural	Inequality
MEANS	Revolution	Communism	Populism	
	War			National (racial) socialism

ground (perhaps because it was out of touch with the exigencies of the modern world, perhaps because it lacked a persuasive, scientific idiom to justify the political authoritarianism required for revolutionary success), while national socialism destroyed itself in the military pursuit of its global objectives. Communism, on the other hand, gained a foothold in Russia, and though it did not attain its global objective, it survived and eventually expanded into a new system of national states. But in order to do so, it had to adjust to the realities of the international system, and as part of this process of adjustment, it had to change its institutions and priorities. While at first the nature and the dimensions of this change were haphazard and not easily discernible, in time they aroused legitimate interest and provided an intellectual rationale for the rise of a new subfield of the social sciences, the field of Communist studies, or, more popularly, of comparative communism.

Not all studies of communism, to be sure, are the work of social scientists, that is, of people who are interested in explanation and prediction by analogy. Nor, for that matter, are most studies of communism studies of social or political change. Indeed, the very opposite may be the case, for given the relative inaccessibility of the subject, a large number of social scientists have been preoccupied by trying to figure out how the system works, not how and why it changes. From these efforts the diverse "models" of Soviet and Communist politics emerged, each trying to isolate some set of elements that it presents as "quintessential" to the understanding of Communist society and government.[2] These models are as illuminating as they are controversial, but they will be discussed here only to the extent that they bear on the subject of the essay, that is, political change.

Mainline Theories

In the context of communism, the subject of political change raises two questions. First, why did communism make its appearance in the history of the modern world and in the history of particular countries? Second, how, why, and under what impulses have the ideological and institutional expressions of communism changed, or how are they likely to change, over time? To these questions various authors have given different answers, either because they approached the subject with different assumptions or because they extrapolated their answers from different historical situations. The differences may be sharply drawn or may be concealed within the theory. But in either case they allow us to distinguish among three major schools of thought, represented by totalitarian, devolutionist, and evolutionist, or developmental, theories of change.

TOTALITARIANISM

The systematic study of Communist government goes back to the years immediately following World War II. At that time, inquiry into the nature of communism was part of a broader endeavor to understand the phenomenon of dictatorship in the twentieth century, to isolate its unique characteristics, or, less sweepingly, to pinpoint differences between traditional and modern forms of tyranny. Out of this endeavor there emerged various models of modern dictatorship, emphasizing the element of total regimentation or, alternatively, the *pursuit* of total control over others. This pursuit implies the rejection of all restraints on the system's behavior, not only the restraints of law and institutions, but the restraints of conventional morality as well. The term "totalitarian" to designate such a dictatorship was conveniently, if somewhat boastfully, provided by Benito Mussolini.

Some of these studies, including a popular volume by Friedrich and Brzezinski, and an earlier volume of essays edited by Friedrich, are essentially descriptive and contain no theory of change.[3] Both of these volumes identify "syndromes," common denominators, and aspects of totalitarianism, such as terror, personalized leadership, economic regimentation, party rule, propaganda, and ideology, but they fail to assign weight to these variables or to explain the relationships among them. Nor do they give us significant clues to the origins of these systems, beyond some vague hints concerning the role of industrialism and modern technology. Still, in their own days these volumes were useful because they laid out somewhat systematically the differences between national socialism and communism on the one hand and, on the other, the more familiar forms of authoritarianism of an earlier age.

Other writers of this totalitarian school go one step further and attempt to link totalitarianism to strains in the social structure and in the psychological makeup of the individual. The most important representative of this school is Hannah Arendt,[4] who, under the influence of the pessimistic schools of European sociology, explains the origins of totalitarianism with reference to social disorganization, alienation, and anomie. More specifically, Arendt places the blame for totalitarianism at the doorsteps of industrialism and its dynamics, which are likely to transform well-structured classes into "masses" and "mobs."[5] Members of these "mobs" have lost orientation in society and, to use Smith's idiom, all vestiges of "fellow feeling." They are "wanderers of the void" who seek to cope with their weightlessness and loss of identity by seeking total domination over others. Terror and other forms of outrage thus become existential acts that help the individual to maintain an element of psychological equilibrium by feverish, violent, and outer-directed activity. Ideology here has no independent existence. It becomes a mere cloak and mask for the resolution of inner conflicts. The politics of totalitarianism is the politics of fleeing anxiety, a functional substitute for psychotherapy, not the pursuit of self-interest.

Others, like Norman Cohn and J. L. Talmon,[6] apply Durkheim's sociological insights to a variety of pre-industrial, premodern situations and relate totalitarianism to stress generated not only by social dislocations but also by all kinds of natural and man-made calamities—plagues, famine, overpopulation, war, and foreign domination. Different as they are, each of these instances generates anxiety, which people escape by taking refuge in fantasy, specifically in the fantasy of terrestrial salvation, the common denominator between medieval chiliasm and modern totalitarianism. To some students of totalitarianism this may be merely a nuance when compared to Arendt's treatment of psychodynamics. But in fact there are significant differences between this theory and Arendt's, for in the theory of Cohn, ideology is not a mere cloak and mask but a social force in its own right, with an impact on collective behavior. Cohn's chiliastic ideologies are thus worth studying, for they presumably tell us what the actor will do next, and since they constitute genuine beliefs, they do provide a logic for the construction of political regimes.

Unlike the early models of Friedrich and Brzezinski, these socio-psychological explanations provide us with a dynamic model of communism. They not only describe the elements of the system; they also give clues as to its rise. But although the models are dynamic, they predict continuity and not change. For within their sociological and psychological framework, social disorganization remains essentially a one-way street. Arendt's totalitarian cannot stop his drive to dominate, for if he stops, his personality structure may collapse. In a like manner, Cohn's true believer will hold on to his belief in terrestrial paradise, for the only alternative to belief is suicide. Totalitarianism is, therefore, destined to be immune to transformation, short of military defeat. Thus although we encounter in this literature a leader and his *Gefolgschaft*, we see no hint of a process of *Vergemeinschaftung* or *Vergesellschaftung*. When and where elements of change manifest themselves, they are construed as signs of temporary relaxation, emergency measures, and tactical retreats. Thus, writing in 1958, Arendt drew a sharp distinction between events in the satellite countries, where totalitarianism had not yet had the time to establish itself firmly, and the Soviet Union, where totalitarianism was firmly in control and where only the means, and not the ends, were thought to have changed. In Arendt's words, "what Stalin achieved by means of a permanent revolution and periodic gigantic purges, Khrushchev hopes to achieve by new devices, built into, so to speak, the social structure itself and meant to assure atomization from within."[7] This view was revised somewhat in the 1968 edition of *Origins of Totalitarianism*, though even this text cautions the reader that "today we [still] cannot know if the process is final . . . [or represents] a mere temporary relaxation."[8]

More or less the same may be said about cultural theories of totalitarianism that explain the phenomenon, not by social and personal disorganization, but by habits and traits that are independent of or outside the social and economic structure. The definition of culture varies from author to author. While some see it as the product of the idiosyncratic confluence of historical events, others describe it as the reflection of the psyche of a nation, ðr of the particular group that has created and shaped the totalitarian movement.[9] Whichever concept they choose as an explanatory construct, culture is presented as a constant, not as a variable: "once a Russian, always a Russian" is the motto that most succinctly expresses this intellectual posture, projecting the image of an unchanging totalitarian regime. First adopted by students of national socialism after World War I, this stance was quickly taken up by students of Communist government during the first years of the Cold War. At that time they rediscovered "eternal Russia,"[10] or the Russian "distrust of the West, the cult of the precedence of the community over the individual, the recognition of unlimited power of governmental authority over society"[11] behind the structure and functioning of Soviet government. The popularity of these theories peaked in the 1950's. Thereafter it declined, only to be resuscitated by some writers to explain various facets of Soviet international behavior.[12]

DEVOLUTION: A NEO-WEBERIAN THEORY

Ironically, the popularity of the theories of totalitarianism—both cultural and sociological—reached a high-water mark in the years after the death of Stalin. The volumes associated with the names of Friedrich and Brzezinski, for instance, were published in the years 1954–56, and the flow of books and articles on the subject of totalitarianism continued for some time thereafter, as dissertations, symposia, and other scholarly efforts reached publication stage. By this time, however, the winds of change were blowing from the Communist orbit, and social scientists had to find ways to deal with those changes within the frame of reference of their own discipline. One such framework was presented by Durkheim, whose concept of anomie had become both a starting and a terminal point of analysis, at least in the sociology of the great pessimists of the age like Hannah Arendt. But for the intellectual community of the United States this was not the age of Durkheim but the age of Weber. In the 1950's and 1960's the popularity of the German master was certainly unmatched by that of other classical social scientists (including Marx, who had not yet found his new generation of followers). Weber, as noted earlier, was sensitive to the problem of social disorganization and aware of the importance of extraordinary and stressful human situations. Unlike Durkheim, however, he did not regard the extraordinary and the anomic as steady states, but rather as high points from which societies might eventually descend to a plateau of normality. It is in this sense that we can describe Weberian approaches to change in Communist systems as devolutionary rather than evolutionary.

The Weberian concept of society has three implications for the study of communism. First, if we accept the validity of the concept, then, much like Durkheim or Arendt, we have to treat communism as a movement that was born out of crisis, social disorganization, and the collapse of traditional norms. Second, and as a corollary, ideology must be seen as a reflection of this crisis. In other words, it is not merely the cloak and mask for the pursuit of naked self-interest, but a set of goals which, whether rational or not, is accepted as valid and is acted upon, if only to gratify some deeply felt need. Third, in its initial stages at least, the Communist movement is best seen as an analogue of Weber's charismatic sect. Like the latter, the underground party is in essence a *Gefolgschaft*, gathered around a forceful figure in the pursuit of a "higher" objective and, for this reason, oblivious to the dictates of economic rationality, or "pragmatism," as well as to conventional legal, moral, and social restraints. This, in turn, explains the "fluidity," shapelessness, and inherent instability of revolutionary regimes. Instability, of course, implies the probability of change. Thus in the long run, much like the Weberian sect, a Communist party must either perish or adapt to the environment by routinizing the leader's charisma and by rationally reordering its priorities.

In perusing the relevant literature, we find the first full-fledged application of these categories in Barrington Moore's two path-breaking volumes published in the 1950's.[13] In them, Moore's analysis proceeds from the familiar Weberian assumption that power in society can be held, exercised, and institutionalized in three ways: as an expression of tradition, as an expression of rational-technical principles, and as an expression of charisma. In the first type of order, decisions are made on the basis of precedent, and political succession operates through the family or kinship system. In the second, power is granted to those who possess technical-managerial expertise. And in the third instance, power is exercised in the name of the "higher" purposes of the ideology, and political positions are distributed on the basis of personal and political loyalties.

The Communist systems of Moore's time corresponded to this third type and displayed both the strengths and weaknesses associated with it in Weberian sociology. The most obvious strength of the system was its ability to pursue a wide range of social goals, including "forced draft" industrialization, ruthlessly and with no regard to human cost. But in its arbitrariness and ruthlessness, the system had damaged its long-range viability and effectiveness. Most significantly, constant meddling by political authorities undermined the efficiency of the economic system, and power exercised by political loyalists resulted in the destruction of a whole generation of technical and military experts. Inherently unstable, Moore felt, the system faced a choice between extinction and change in the direction of either traditionalism or technological-managerial competence. To put it differently, proceeding from the Weberian hypothesis, Moore was ready to predict a transfer of power from the personal cronies of the chief either to the managers of industry or to the traditionally oriented, nationalistic military elite. Written in the years 1949–54, Moore's studies show remarkable insight into the dynamics of Soviet politics. Indeed, they are among the few written in that period that actually predict, rather than register, political change.

Another attempt to apply Weberian categories to the establishment and dynamics of Communist regimes was made by Samuel P. Huntington, in an introduction to a series of essays largely devoted to illustrating the validity of the hypotheses discussed above.[14] In these essays, including Huntington's own, communism appears merely as one, albeit quite important, variant of a larger category, that of "revolutionary one-party" regimes. All of these regimes, including Communist ones, are viewed through the Weberian prism: they are characterized by "personalized leadership, particularly of the charismatic type," and as a consequence suffer from certain internal contradictions and debilities that, in the long run, propel them toward a more "formalized and institutionalized" form of political existence.[15]

As in the works of Weber and Moore, revolutionary movements are the products of social crisis, and their ideology is to be taken seriously. But over time the movements will encounter, indeed create, new contingencies beyond the initial social crisis. One of these stems from the movements' very success, which makes their ideology irrelevant and tends to deprive them of their original raison d'être.[16] The other, and still greater, threat to the stability of these movements stems from the imperatives of resolving the problem of succession in a milieu of personalized authority and leadership. Adaptation to these contingencies is neither mechanical nor simple. It requires struggle "between the party organization and a Weberian sequence of opponents,"[17] that is, the intelligentsia, the bureaucracy, and the technocrats. But in order to survive, the regime must adapt to "changed circumstances . . . [and to] the needs of a relatively consensual society . . . much as ruling monarchies eventually became constitutional ones."[18]

Whereas Weber's thinking on the subject of change is strictly linear (reflecting the exigencies of survival that push the movement in the direction of institutionalization and routine), the theories of many recent writers are, if only unintentionally, dialectical in character. This is because they invoke contradictions built into the situation with which they deal. Such contradictions are seen to arise between revolutionary ends and means, more specifically between revolutionary ideology and organization. In this respect, two lines of argument may be discerned in the relevant body of writings. One of these pivots around the notions of status, inequality, and vested interests and proceeds through the following sequence of premises and syllogisms: (1) ideology provides a series of concrete, long-term objectives; (2) in order to pursue these effectively, the movement requires organizational instruments; (3) but organizations, by nature, are hierarchies of power, or command structures; (4) such hierarchies have the inherent tendency to transform themselves into hierarchies of status and privilege. Once they do, the amorphous, ideologically committed retinue of the leader will have transformed itself into a new class of *arrivisti*, more interested in entrenched class privilege than in the pursuit of lofty and risky revolutionary objectives. It is in this manner that revolutionary radicalism so often turns into ossified, Thermidorian conservatism. But the dialectic is not only a theory of ossification. It also offers explanations for the nature of Stalinism. For if in the long run it predicts the deradicalization of revolutionary regimes, in the short run it can well accommodate the image of a charismatic leader purging and shaking up his party to maintain the fluidity of the situation and to preserve the revolutionary commitment of the political movement.

It is not generally remembered that the revolutionary dialectic is an idea whose origins go back to the anarchist movements of the nineteenth century. It is from there that the term *arrivismo* entered the vocabulary of Italian fascism. Closer to the present subject, the dialectic inspired Trotsky's observations concerning a "Thermidorian reaction in Russia[19] and Milovan Djilas's thesis concerning the rise of a "new class,"[20] as well as the recent spate of neo-Marxist writings on bureaucratization and "capitalist restoration" in European Communist regimes.[21] But the idea of a revolutionary dialectic has also entered the non-Marxist writings of such "mainstream" writers as Zbigniew Brzezinski, Robert C. Tucker, and Seweryn Bialer, each of whom in different ways tends to relate the "rationalization" or "deradicalization" of these regimes to the elite's tendency to protect its gains, status, and security.[22] To quote Brzezinski, "power like wealth has an inherent tendency to attract strong attachments in those who enjoy it. Consequently, the triumphant elite, while not abandoning its ultimate ends, tends to stress immediate power considerations," which explains why "pressures toward gradualism and stability develop," and why "totalitarianism may become less unpredictable, arbitrary, and [less] openly terroristic."[23]

If one formulation of the revolutionary dialectic centers around the notion of inequality, the other derives from that of functional specialization. Here, the premise and the syllogisms follow more or less this line of reasoning: (1) ideology is an action program; (2) to realize the goals of the action program, the movement requires organization and structure; (3) organization, by definition, implies functional specialization; (4) functional specialization tends to subvert revolutionary commitment to the original goals of the movement because, in the place of "goal consciousness," it breeds "role consciousness." Put the revolutionary cadre in charge of a factory or transportation system, and he will begin to think like a manager, less concerned with the future of world revolution than with schedules and balances of account. In this manner, the revolution will be drowned in trivia and pettiness.

While some facets of this argument are by no means alien to "bourgeois" social psychology, they were recently brought into sharper focus by the Chinese cultural revolution of the 1960's and Mao's own acute concerns with bureaucratization and revolutionary purity.[24] It is possibly for this reason that while the dialectics of inequality have flourished among students of European communism, the dialectics of role and function were brought to the discipline by China scholars, most explicitly by Chalmers Johnson.[25] Like others under this general rubric, Johnson traces the rise of the movement to "societies plagued by incoherence," that is, by social disorganization and stress.[26] Thus again, ideology is not the mere cloak and mask for self-interest but a social force in its own right, the basis of a genuine "goal culture," which in the name of egalitarian and humanistic objectives "elicits purposive revolutionary behavior and sacrifice for a significant part of the revolutionary party."[27]

The contradiction arises precisely because the revolutionary ideology is a genuine belief system that imposes obligations and calls for concrete steps for implementation. Thus while the "Communist goal culture does not aim at a 'modernized society,'" the successful pursuit of the ultimate purposes of the movement requires the building of a modern industrial base.[28] This gives rise to a new "transfer culture," shaped by industrial norms and managerial role playing. The end result is "bureaucratization . . . [that] leaders of a totalitarian mobilization regime can never fully control," for "the mounting pressures to address the system's basic imbalance lead to mounting resistance from the bureaucracies created by the mobilization effort."[29] The outcome of this struggle is far from predetermined: the conflict between the goal and transfer cultures may flare up time and again, and a revolutionary system may destroy itself in a series of increasingly violent confrontations. Still, in the long run, the cards seem to be stacked against the goal culture, for the exigencies of sheer survival force elites to address "the functional requisites of the social system," and to reduce the revolutionary vision to purely ritualistic and symbolic functions.[30] When this occurs, a significant threshold has been passed: the stage is set for the routinization, normalization, or institutionalization of the revolutionary regime.

DEVELOPMENT: ECONOMIC, SOCIAL, AND POLITICAL

If the above theories conceptualize change as "devolution," or transition from the extraordinary to the ordinary, the third major school of Communist studies describes the process in evolutionary, or developmental, terms—that is, as progress from lower to higher stages, whether in the economic or the political sphere. In contrast to neo-Durkheimian and neo-Weberian thinking, these theories do not emphasize escape from psychological or social strain but the rational calculation of gain. In other words, they belong to the category of interest theories. As such, their ultimate inspiration comes from the great optimists of the eighteenth and nineteenth centuries. For the purposes of Communist studies, this mode of thinking was resuscitated in the early post-Stalin period and since then has been a major competitor to devolutionist theories in the comparative study of economic and political change.

As the title of this section indicates, developmental theories of Communism may be classified under three subheadings. Economic theories of development will be familiar from our discussions in Chapter 3 of the problems of Third World countries.[31] The assumption underlying them is that in order to survive as autonomous and organized entities, the societies of the periphery need to generate a measure of material progress. In principle at least, they may choose among several strategies to accomplish the task. They may, for instance, opt for a market economy with a conciliatory political system or for a more authoritarian form of government, justified by traditional values and objectives. Alternatively, they may opt for the all-out mobilization of their resources, which requires a "consummatory" ideology to legitimate coercion and rigid regimentation. The historical role of communism is to provide such an ideology. By doing so, communism loses its uniqueness and becomes "merely part of a larger process of modernization."[32] To some writers, like John Kautsky and

Robert C. Tucker, this is merely a historical accident: for while its millenarian vision makes Marxism eminently suitable as an ideology of mobilization, they remind us that the original purposes of the movement had little to do with modernization or development.[33] To others, however, Marxism, or its Leninist variety, is nothing but an ideology of development, a thin cloak over the desire of peripheral elites to raise their countries from the condition of backwardness. Thus, in the words of Theodore von Laue, "the Russian revolution established a new [political] category, the revolution of underdeveloped countries. . . . Underneath the travail of revolution and counterrevolution . . . terror or counterterror, the deeper [historical] necessity took its course. Not always clearly expressed . . . it aimed at the conversion of Russian state and society to modern industrialism."[34] Or, still more explicitly, "from the summer of 1917, [the Bolshevik revolution] was a revolt against backwardness, already foreshadowed in the character of Leninism."[35]

While some writers were content to explain the rise of communism, relating it to the humiliations and deprivations of backwardness, others have used the developmental frame of reference to explain and anticipate changes in the structure of established Communist governments. The logic of the argument here is engagingly simple, hence its considerable popularity among the students of communism. In order to mobilize the manpower and resources of a backward society, so the argument goes, communism must resort to terror, propaganda, and personalized leadership. But as the task of mobilization is accomplished, "a progressively decreasing proportion of the population needs to be subjected to terror or to heavy-handed regimentation."[36] But then the "primitive magic" of charismatic leadership slowly outlives its usefulness and comes into conflict with the "new needs" of the situation.[37] In Russia, for instance, the "phenomenal growth" of national income (from 1930 to 1950) made it possible for the regime to "soften class privileges." Political orthodoxy, the iron curtain, and the "elaborate mythology" of Marxism-Leninism had by 1953 become not only superfluous but "socially useless."[38] Carried ad extremum, the argument produced a theory of convergence that envisaged a common political future for all industrial societies. More carefully formulated, the theory merely anticipates the rise of a more predictable and orderly, if still tightly regimented, society, in which "systems management" takes precedence over developmental objectives.[39]

Like most economic theories of development, sociological theories of development were not originally formulated in the context of Communist societies. Rather, these theories were devised by students of industrial societies in the Occident and were then transferred into the domain of Communist studies in an attempt to invigorate them. The emphasis in all of these theories is on technology and innovation—the increased use of inanimate implements and sources of energy—and on the consequent differentiation and functional specialization of society. For the political scientist, these theories raise, and try to answer, questions concerning the impact of innovation and differentiation on the social structure.[40]

As we have seen in Chapter 2, the answers to these questions tend to be optimistic. In the mainstream of political sociology, Levy, Parsons, Kerr, Harbison, Moore, and others[41] emphasize the increasing similarity of industrial societies, the convergence of their status systems, the importance of technical expertise, and the compelling political logic of social complexity, all of which tend to point toward diminishing authoritarianism and increasing pluralism. Thus, in the words of Marion Levy, "as the level of modernization increases, the level of structural uniformity among relatively modernized societies [also] increases."[42] Or, in the still more strongly formulated proposition of Clark Kerr, "cultural and national differences are becoming less significant . . . the further the country is along the road toward industrialism."[43] And further, industrial society, "as any established society, develops a distinctive consensus, which relates individuals and groups to each other . . . [in] an open community encouraging occupational and geographical mobility."[44] This society is "pluralistic, with a great variety of associations and groups, and of large-scale operations; the individual is attached to a variety of such groups and organizations,"[45] although Kerr warns that the prevalence of these forms should not imply pluralism in the Western sense.

In sharp contrast to these views, we may point to the works of Bendix, in which he raises doubts about the presumed logic of structural complexity and argues that cultural continuity is as important as change in shaping public authority. While he agrees that industrialism results in structural complexity and that it is likely to mobilize and multiply political actors, he also warns that the behavior of these new elements in politics is likely to be shaped by political tradition, most notably by traditions of immunity, reciprocity, and institutional autonomy. In the absence of these, the modern industrial state will not become democratic, but "plebiscitarian."[46]

Let us then turn to the school of thought that regards communism as an instance, or instrument, of political development. The founder of this school may be said to be Cyril E. Black, whose contributions have been discussed at some length in Chapter 2. Here we need only to recall the implicit functionalism of these writings, and their Parsonian, or Spencerian, emphasis on adaptation to the "challenges" of the external and internal environment. When left unattended, these challenges create strife, crises, and ultimately the demise of society as an organized entity. Contrariwise, when a challenge or task is successfully dealt with, society moves one stage closer to full-fledged membership in the international community. Although Black is not explicit on this point, the tasks can be accomplished in different ways, under different ideological guises, and with different organizational strategies. Communism represents one of these. Thus despite its numerous objectionable features that Black clearly dislikes, communism emerges as a movement for modernization and development and, in the last analysis, as an instrument of social progress by virtue of its ability to create an effective institutional environment for change.

Black's scheme of the stages of political development has been significantly revised and refined by Kenneth Jowitt, a political scientist. His several contributions to the subject, above all his *Revolutionary Breakthroughs*, accept Black's notion of historical contingency and postulate that, as a matter of survival, societies will respond to challenges to their existence by developing modern forms of political organizations and communities.[47] Accordingly, and far more clearly than in Black's historical construct, Jowitt's theory is not one of economic modernization, but of nation building, even though modernization also enters the picture as a goal that elites have to pursue in order to be able to create a viable national community. Like Black's theory, Jowitt's treats modernization as a precondition of integration, or in Jowitt's words of the "inclusion" of various segments of society into a modern political community, in which the individual has a sense of being part of the body politic. Again, as in Black's essay, the imperatives of survival move societies from stage to stage, although such progress is by no means inevitable. Indeed, as formulated by Jowitt, the theory leaves plenty of room for omission or human error. It is thus conceivable that Jowitt's elites may fail to comprehend their historical mission; even if they do comprehend it, they may not exercise correct tactical judgments at the appropriate moment in time. In such instances, there may be regression or stagnation, until an elite arises with a better understanding of the historical situation. But once such an elite arises and successfully acts upon its political insight, a society will indeed move from a lower to a higher stage of development. There, new structural configurations impose new constraints on the actors and make it possible for the observer to discern both typical and optimal forms of political behavior.

What makes Jowitt's work significant is its ability to identify clearly the "Leninist," or revolutionary, path of political development and to juxtapose it clearly with a "reformist," or incrementalist, path. While the latter, by definition, implies accommodation and compromise, including compromise with traditional interest groups hostile to the idea of the modern state and society, Leninists will opt for a strategy of "breakthrough" by revolutionary violence. Such a strategy implies class struggle, the destruction of traditional interest groups, and the atomization of society by terror, which Jowitt postulates to be necessary for the building of an effective political community that can withstand the exigencies of the modern age. Communists may not be the only ones to effect such a breakthrough, but they are uniquely qualified—or, at any rate, better qualified than fascists and populists—by some of the doctrinal and organizational features of their political legacy. One of the key features of this ideology is universalism, which permits Marxist-Leninists to transcend nativist-particularist-populist sentimentality and to carry out ruthlessly the collectivization of agriculture. This measure is pivotal to revolutionary success, not only because it creates economies of scale in the place of an inefficient peasant economy, but also because it creates a new social milieu in which uprooted peasants can be transformed into modern citizens free from traditional-particularistic cultural encumbrances. But this is not all, for Jowitt attributes the success of Leninist breakthroughs to yet another aspect of the ideology: its unique ability to combine affect and impersonality by vesting charisma in the party, a rationally and routinely functioning modern organization. The result of this fusion is revolutionary continuity. As in the instance of Weber's *Amtscharisma*, the founding hero's mantle is easily passed on to a new generation of leadership. If theorists of devolution discern a process of de-radicalization in the experiences of Communist societies, Jowitt, like other developmental theorists, discerns not the decline of radicalism, but the fulfillment of its original objectives.

As an overall theory of change, Jowitt's hypothesis of political development recognizes only two viable roads to the creation of a modern state. One is the liberal road that was built on the great economic revolutions of the Occident in the post-medieval period. This road is described as historically unique: it had been traveled only once, and the experience is not likely to be repeated by any other country. The second road is that of Marxism-Leninism, which starts out in history as a violent response to economic backwardness and political dependence. Critics of Jowitt would discern a number of alternative roads. But to him all of these are mere blind alleys that lead nowhere in history: as long as the societies of the Third World follow the path of reformist incrementalism, they are not likely to emerge as viable national states and equal partners in a highly competitive international system. Still, Marxism-Leninism does not guarantee success either. Although its ideology is suitable for the task of nation building in principle, the success of the movement also requires "congruence" between ideology and "cultural type,"[48] which thus become explanatory variables of the last instance.

It is in the absence of such congruence that we encounter in real life Communist regimes that, while earnest in their commitment, have failed to accomplish a revolutionary breakthrough and have drifted away from the formula of revolutionary violence. The examples of Poland and Yugoslavia are the most striking cases in point. Jowitt is well aware of this, and it is for this reason that categories like neo-traditionalism and corruption have begun to crop up in his more recent writings.[49]

Communism in Global Perspective

While these theorists are "mainline" in the sense that they are preoccupied with the structure of particular societies (and that, like the great classics, they tend to portray change as a linear progression of events), a larger, global perspective is often implicit in their works. This is especially true among writers who, like Theodore von Laue, link the rise of communism to economic backwardness, a condition that, after all, is meaningful only in the larger context of international income inequality and as a reverse mirror image of occidental progress. Few of these writers, to be sure, appear to subscribe to a zero-sum view of the relationship between development and decay, and certainly none are as explicit in developing the world system concept as Wallerstein, Anderson, or Skocpol. But most of them explain the rise of communism (in Russia and elsewhere on the world periphery) with reference to social tensions and configurations characteristic of underdeveloped regions or "dependent" political entities: the progressive impoverishment of the peasantry, the relative deprivations of the urban working class, declining employment opportunities for the educated, and the ever-increasing use of state power to skew the pattern of income distribution in favor of the political and social elite. What needs to be stated more emphatically is that these conditions did not emanate from the societies themselves, but reflected the crisis of the larger modern world system and the failure of its distributive mechanisms to correct the more serious problem of international income inequality. It was within the context of this larger crisis that Leninist movements became rebellions not only against the inequities of particular societies—like Tsarist Russia or imperial China—but also against the existing global division of labor and resources.

The relevance of the larger, global picture is also recognized by authors who write about the shift from Leninism to Stalinism. The explanation here is usually framed in terms of contradictions between "ideology and power" (Brzezinski) or between the "goal" and "transfer" cultures (Johnson). But again these dichotomies become meaningful only within the context of the larger international system and its competitive pressures. After all, historically it was the prevalence of these pressures that made Communist systems "postpone" or "ritualize" (Moore) their revolutionary objectives, or, perhaps more accurately, formulate a synthesis between revolution and development. For while the logic of power dictated the policies of forced-draft industrialization, the logic of revolutionary salvationism provided justification for a thoroughly ruthless pursuit of the economic objectives. It is on account of this ability to abandon all legal and moral restraints that Stalinism may be described as "totalitarian." It is also in this sense that we can discern significant continuities between Leninism and Stalinism: though the priorities of the Soviet regime changed over time, the ideological justification for the priorities remained the same.

While these aspects of the larger global picture are at least implicit in the literature on communism, another consequence of international inequality—the demonstration effect of the advanced nations—has been on the whole neglected by the students of the Communist world. The few authors who recognize the existence of an IDE tend to downplay its importance.[50] Still, even after a cursory examination of the total evidence, one can hardly remain unimpressed by the weight of this factor and by the continuity of the pressures that Western material standards placed on the institutions and stability of these regimes. Thus, from the 1920's through the 1950's the IDE, perhaps more than any other factor, was responsible for the extreme insularity of the Stalinist regime and for its withdrawal, not only from global markets (as Wallerstein asserts[51]), but from the global material civilization created by Western progress. The purpose of this relatively successful insulation was to reduce potential consumer demand on scarce resources, needed for the rapid development of the economy.

The institutionalization of the purge during the same period may likewise be related to the noxious influences of the more developed capitalist countries. For while the masses could more or less effectively be insulated from contamination, the elites, even in the totalitarian milieu of the Soviet state, had to serve as a link to the outside world. To those who still remember her, Garbo's Ninotchka makes this point. It is thus not unreasonable to suggest that campaigns of vigilance and the permanent purge were methods to combat the threat of elite contamination. That more was involved than Stalin's personal paranoia or the Russian cultural tradition (with its "pathological suspicion" of foreigners) is amply demonstrated by the fact that methods of physical isolation and purges have not been restricted to Soviet Communism, but have been part and parcel of the methods of rule by all other European and Asian Communist governments. The "bamboo curtain" and the cultural revolution of Mao's China are the most obvious cases in point.

In the long run, of course, these measures generate their own costs, which may even exceed the benefits. When this happens, pressures begin to operate against terror and insularity, and for the "softening" of the regime. That this softening is supported by the very members of the elite should by no means be surprising. At a convenient moment—which may arrive upon the death of the revolutionary despot—the regime may begin to open up, while the elite turns into a new class by acquiring immunities and privileges. This is, of course, what happened in the Soviet Union and Eastern Europe after the death of Stalin and is being repeated in China in the post-Mao period. Once this happens, however, the Communist society reenters the magnetic field of global material civilization, and elites will rapidly succumb to the lures of status consumption; that is to say, they will attempt to raise their material standards to the level set by their counterparts in the core countries.[52] Some of this consumption is legal and institutionalized in the forms of special bonuses and opportunities, but in an economy of scarcities these opportunities are likely to be limited; hence very soon corruption becomes rampant, particularly at the middle echelon of party, economic, and state managers.[53] In other words, in the absence of massive terror, insulation, and the purges, Communist society begins to face the same problems of economic backwardness as the other nations of the periphery. If the concept of convergence is meaningful at all, it is more with respect to the future of Communist and Third World countries than to that of the Western and the Communist orbits.

The larger problem, of course, is that the IDE vitiates the positive effects of development and relativizes the accomplishments of planned economic change. Here we must stop for a moment to recall that Communist societies, particularly in Europe, have been quite successful in creating infrastructure and generating change. While the exact figures may remain in doubt, few experts would question that these societies have increased the per capita product between two and three times over the past 40 years. This is a respectable accomplishment when compared to the past, as well as when compared to most of the "developing" countries of the non-European world. But frustratingly, in the same period of time Russia's share in the planetary product has barely changed, and the ratio of Soviet and American gross national products experienced but a three percent increase for the former, from 42 to 45 percent, between 1900 and 1978.[54] As to the ratio between East and West Europe, preliminary calculations indicate that for East Europe it changed by less than 5 percent, from 35.8 to 40.3 percent of West Europe's between 1926 and 1978.[55] The fact of the matter is that while Communist economies have been developing at a respectable rate, Western economies have been developing still faster. The goal of "catching up" has thus remained an elusive one for Communist governments. The Stalinist regimes may have accomplished breakthroughs in other respects, but they have not changed the relative backwardness of their societies within the larger picture of the world economy. Polish, Hungarian, and Czech workers may live today far better than their parents and grandparents did and are certainly better housed and more healthy, but they are far from acquiring a standard that has become a "staple of decency" for their counterparts in Western societies. As a result, the sense of relative deprivation in these countries is as salient as it was half a century ago, and the management of these deprivations requires as much skill as the actual planning for economic change.

In the light of this, we may question the validity of the popular hypothesis that sees "development" replacing "utopian" globalistic designs in the thinking of Communist elites. No doubt the hypothesis was first inspired by the obsession of the Khrushchev years with "overtaking" the advanced capitalist countries. The more recent experiments of China with an avowed policy of modernization may add new grist to the developmental mill. But the proponents of the hypothesis overlook the fact that, in the long run, development has not been less utopian than the pursuit of a new global order, by revolutionary or military means.

Thus, though the gaze of scholarship is still too much fixed on Communist economic strategies and their implications for Communist states, the failure to close the gap between themselves and the capitalist world may augur not more, but less, emphasis on development. Indeed, if we examine the priorities and identity of contemporary Communist regimes across the world, we will find a good number among them that today question the idea of industrialization as a viable strategy for solving the problems of humanity, as well as of their own national states. The seeds of this doubt were first sown by Mao, and they have since received doctrinal support by all shades of radical scholarship, in works that argue once again the impossibility of building socialist societies in the context of a capitalist world economy.[56] The argument is echoed by those who, like Pol Pot, fear cultural contamination more than the imperialism of trade. Thus while the elites of China have recently embraced both modernization and consumerism, those of a number of Communist movements in Latin America and Asia have all but abandoned the developmental option and are returning to the populist ideal of equality in the midst of bucolic simplicity.

The study of major Communist nations, above all, that of the

Soviet Union, meanwhile presents a different challenge. Here, the question is not whether the global perspective has been rediscovered but whether it has ever been truly abandoned by the elite. The fact of the matter is that great powers cannot easily abandon external commitments, a circumstance that the developmentalist approach to Communism has largely ignored in recent decades. In the case of Communist nations, the universalist idiom of earlier times may easily be adjusted to justify these great power commitments and to infuse them with dynamism. But if the idiom is alive, its meanings have undergone change: the pursuit of global objectives has become "routinized," that is, their pursuit has been subjected to certain rules of the game. Its prime instrument now is statecraft and not revolutionary mobilization. Still more significantly, Soviet elites seem to have adjusted themselves to the "hard realities" of the human condition, believing that long after the universal advent of socialism, the more advanced Communist nations would have to exercise tutelage over their less experienced brethren. The Soviet image of the world today is one of hierarchy and power, devoid of the egalitarianism of early Marxism and Leninism.

These are significant conceptual thresholds. They may not yet have been consciously crossed, but signs that they might be abound and have induced at least one writer to speak of "the Russian New Right,"[57] whose ideology is more akin to that of fascism than to that of original communism. At the same time, we are inclined to dub Asian and Latin American Communists as populists, mainly because of their Maoist distrust of modern material civilization. This language may, admittedly, overstate the point. But it reflects the looming crisis of contemporary communism, not as a political movement, nor as an imperial system, but as an ideology that once gave the movement an identity so distinctly different from other radical movements of both Left and Right.

FIVE

The Passing of Industrial Society

Two Views of Industrialism

To go back to a point made earlier in this essay, there are substantial differences in the ways in which contemporary scholarship has set out to conceptualize the nature of the modern world system. But next to these, we should remember, there are also significant common denominators among these approaches, which set them apart from conventional sociological theories of development. Thus whether they are Marxist or not, these theories proceed from the assumption that the prime sources of tension in the modern world are economic scarcity and regional income disparity. Just as significantly, the theories take a zero-sum view of global reality. For although not all theories subscribe to the view that the progress of the Occident has been achieved at the expense of the rest, they all seem to agree that, in one way or another, the rise of modern industrialism in the West has been, despite its many advantages, the source of considerable trouble for the societies of the rest of the world.

But what about industrial societies? Do they represent the ne plus ultra of progress, the terminal stage of history in which, as Marx suggested, there will be no politics and no social change? Or will they continue to differentiate and hence to develop in cheerful open-endedness, as Spencer assumed, ever improving their capacity to adapt to the challenges of their external environment? Or are they harbingers of anomie and personal disorganization as Weber and Durkheim portrayed the future in their darker moments? These questions have not ceased to haunt political sociologists in this century. But since the great classical writers were ambivalent, and since history itself provided ambiguous answers, scholarship, too, has continued to waver between abject pessimism and exuberant optimism.

The political sociology of the interwar period, existing under the dual shadow of European fascism and communism, was of the first variety. Indeed, it was on the whole more pessimistic about the chances of an industrial civilization than were its precursors in the nineteenth century. Thus whereas Weber and Durkheim in their own time could still see a glimmer of hope beyond the iron cage, some of their disciples and successors, like Karl Mannheim and Jose Ortega, saw modern industrialism as a blind alley, a point of no return in history. It is true that this generation, too, continued to equate industrialism with mastery. But its social scientists shared a despair at what they perceived to be a grand disjuncture, or "general disproportion,"[1] between this mastery and the lack of progress with respect to other aspects of collective existence. According to Mannheim, this disproportion had two dimensions. First, there was the gap between the process of "fundamental democratization," whereby an increasing number of people develop a sense of their power, and the growing complexity of industrial society, which prevents the average person from acquiring real insight into the social mechanism.[2] Second, there was the disjuncture between "functional" and "substantive" rationality, the ability of large-scale organizations to interrelate cost and benefit versus the ability of individuals to reflect about ultimate ends and thereby to make intelligent social choices for themselves.[3] In a somewhat similar vein, Ortega bemoaned the gap between the rising political efficacy and the declining insight of the masses in an age of "technicism," which he defined as industrialism plus scientific experiment.[4] In neither one of these formulations was there much hope left for a civic polity. If Mannheim believed that industrialism would transform democracy into a form of bureaucratic absolutism in which mindless robots followed orders of technicians, Ortega expected the dissolution of liberal democracy into anarchy.

The whole tenor of inquiry changed in the years following World War II. The center of gravity in social studies shifted to the United States, a country that, much like Spencer's England a century before, was the leading industrial power of the world, virtually dizzy with its own success. In this atmosphere, the gloom of Mannheim or Ortega had very little appeal. The badge of accomplishment was granted to those who could capture the exuberant mood of a society that held up its own experience as a model for the whole world to imitate, and in order to earn that badge, the academic mainstream returned to the sociological millenarianism of the nineteenth century. Once again, this implied the resuscitation of Marx, whose economic theory of history would provide intellectual underpinnings for a new utopianism concerning the advent of a final, mass consumption stage of history. The few surviving pessimists who, like Erich Fromm and Hannah Arendt, were faithfully carrying forward the sociological tradition of Mannheim and Durkheim, remained odd persons out, more appreciated for style than for substance. At any rate, their works were less influential than the writings of those who, like Ralf Dahrendorf and Daniel Bell, were predicting, in the Spencerian fashion, the "decreasing intensity and violence in industrial society," the "institutionalization of class conflict,"[5] and the "end of ideology."[6]

Perhaps still more characteristic of the general air of optimism was the way in which some of the great doomsayers of yesteryear became theorists of progress, celebrating modern industrialism. Thus whereas Durkheim himself gloomily pondered the rise of dictatorship or the anomie of industrialism, modern Durkheimians hypothesized that the politics of mass society "might go both ways," that the potential for dictatorship might be deflected by the prevalence of civic associations that "not only protects elites and non-elites from one another but does so in a manner that permits liberal democratic control,"[7] as in the case of the United States. In a very similar manner, Mannheim's modern man, who had a sense of power but no intelligent insight into the social mechanism, now has come to be seen as an informed and trusted participant with a marked sense of personal efficacy and with beliefs in a "reasonably lawful world under human control," a perspective acquired by "participation in a large-scale modern productive enterprise such as the factory."[8] And, perhaps as an ultimate irony, Weber's modern man, "this specialist without spirit, this sensualist without heart . . . this nullity who imagines that it has attained a level of civilization never before achieved,"[9] now reappeared on the scene as a successful architect of just such a civilization, with a virtually unlimited capacity to produce and to absorb change, who, instead of being confined in an iron cage, was now portrayed as a person passing "from rigidity and closed mindedness . . . toward flexibility and cognitive openness," without suffering from the adverse consequences of personal or cultural maladjustment.[10]

The Coming of Post-Industrial Society

This optimism about the prospects of industrial society, however, received a severe jolt in the mid-1960's. It was only five or six years after the publication of a spate of major works—by Bell, Dahrendorf, and Rostow—extolling the virtues of industrialism, that the "advanced" societies of the Occident, supposedly peaceful, restrained, and pluralistic, became engulfed in a political crisis that entailed violent demonstrations, urban terrorism, and guerrilla warfare, all in the name of ideology. Rather than bargaining over their proper share of the collective pie, radical groups set out to change the very rules of the game in ways that just a few years before were inconceivable to political sociologists. This experience was clearly at variance with received wisdom and prompted a search for a new paradigm within which the crisis of industrialism could be properly explained.

In the normal course of events such a crisis in received wisdom produces a new generation of revisionist scholars, and in the process of revision the practitioners of older schools gradually disappear. Part of them become converts, "others cling to one or another of the older views and they are simply read out of the profession."[11] Not in this particular instance, however, for some of the revisionists were members of the sociological establishment and had also been leading proponents of the old industrial society hypothesis. This circumstance is well reflected in the results of the intellectual enterprise, for out of the intellectual crisis the old paradigm reemerged, not tainted, but still further corroborated. Industrial society, so this revisionist argument ran, *was* inherently peaceful and conducive to political pluralism. What the turmoil of the 1960's showed was not the failure of industrial society to live up to the expectations of liberal sociology, but rather the possibility of development beyond industrialism, toward a new "post-industrial" stage. For one reason or another, this stage was less conducive to democracy than the stage of industrialism. And even if, in the long run, the problems of a post-industrial society might be dealt with effectively, for the time being, the societies of the Occident found themselves between two stages, plagued by the disequilibrium between the new structure and old institutions that obtains during periods of intensive change.

This generalized argument is vintage Spencer, with some elements borrowed from Marx. In any case, it is well within the dominant sociological perspective of the previous decades. Thus, in Morris Janowitz's words, "the social stratification of an advanced industrial society is best understood in terms of the division of labor, that is, by occupational categories."[12] As in the classical formulations of macro-sociology, the sources of change are seen to be endogenous, and little attention is paid to the global division of labor or to trans-societal sources of political change. Also, consistently with the classical formula, we are provided with a three-tiered paradigm, or in Janowitz's words a "three-step agenda for research," in which the "point of entrance is to investigate the ecological-technological-economic structure of social organization . . . the intermediate step is to explore interactive processes which create societal institutions," and the final step is "the analysis of elites, power, and decision-making processes."[13]

The test of the paradigm, of course, will require some demonstration of the existence of linkages among the different tiers of the construct, above all, between the new "post-industrial" configurations and the "weakness" of the political regimes. Why does industrialism sustain democracy, and why does post-industrialism produce the very opposite result? In an attempt to provide the linkage, Janowitz seems to hark back to Mannheim's pessimism, suggesting that "changes in social stratification and the growth of the welfare state make it more difficult for the individual and his household to calculate enlightened self-interest and group interest. The result is that the citizen and his household have chronic difficulty in aggregating and expressing political preferences by the alternatives posed in periodic national elections."[14] Thus, "during a continuing period of deficit national economy, these groupings increase their demands for collective economic aid and governmental benefits,"[15] creating intolerable pressures for the system. The problem is one of relative scarcity created by the lack of adequate understanding, which in turn has been created by the growing complexity of the social mechanism. The same argument, of course, has been used both pro and con the viability of a civic polity. For if Mannheim believed that complexity would undermine the "intelligent insight" of the participants, Spencer and Smith had been convinced that such complexity virtually mandated political civility.

Bell's *The Coming of Post-Industrial Society* is cast in the same conceptual mold, but its treatment of linkages between social and political variables is still more ambiguous. To begin with, though ambitious in scope, the work also displays considerable epistemological diffidence. We are told, for instance, that in a complex world it is well-nigh impossible to identify cause and effect, and that the best we can hope to accomplish is to pinpoint certain "axial principles and structures in an effort to specify not causation . . . but centrality . . . within a conceptual schema or organizing frame around which the other institutions are draped [and provide] an energizing principle that is the primary logic for the others."[16] Bell also denies that changes in the social structure "determine" corresponding changes in the polity or culture.[17] Yet once we cut through the verbal underbrush of this argument, the outlines of the old, nineteenth-century paradigm emerge quite clearly. The "axial principle," or independent variable, is technology; the intervening variable is the social structure; and the dependent variables are political institutions and consciousness. Thus "the sources of the upheaval are scientific and technological."[18] The "concept of post-industrial society emphasizes the centrality of theoretical knowledge, the axis around which new technology, economic growth, and the stratification of society will be organized."[19] The book deals primarily with the way "in which the economy is being transformed and the occupational system reworked."[20] Changes in the social structure then "pose questions" and "management problems for the political system."[21] They "enlarge and complicate modes of decision-making."[22] "The relationship between the social structure and the political order becomes one of the chief problems in a post-industrial society."[23] Finally, the new society creates new modes of life, and "the new modes of life, which depend on the primacy of cognitive and theoretical knowledge, inevitably challenge the tendencies of culture."[24]

A third study cast in the framework of post-industrialism is Zbigniew Brzezinski's *Between Two Ages*. This volume, perhaps even more so than Janowitz's or Bell's, is firmly rooted in the reductionist traditions of the nineteenth century. Once again, the pivotal concept of the study is technology, the dynamics of which is the demiurge of change moving societies from one historical stage to another. Just as Marx's handloom produced feudalism, and his power loom produced capitalism, so Brzezinski's computers and telecommunication devices produce a new "technetronic" age. In his own words, the advanced countries of the world "are beginning to emerge from the industrial stage of development [and] are entering an age in which technology, and especially electronics, . . . are increasingly becoming the principal determinants of social change, altering the mores, the social structure, the values and the global outlook of society."[25] Or, even more explicitly formulated, the technetronic society "is one that is shaped culturally, psychologically, socially and economically by the impact of technology."[26] Except for the terminology, this is the old relationship between base and superstructure.

But although this book shares the reductionism of other writings on post-industrialism, it does not share their structural, or systemic, parochialism. It is true that, like Bell and Janowitz, Brzezinski focuses on the process of technological innovations in the advanced societies of the world, above all, the United States. But it is also true that he is fully cognizant of the worldwide implications of these changes and of the "paradox of the age" that progress in one sector of the world becomes the cause of decay in others. The key to the paradox is the sense of relative deprivation that is generated by images of wealth in the Western countries.[27] It is because of the IDE that today's humanity lives, not in a global village of harmony, but in a global city of conflict.

If the problems of the larger world system are the products of relative scarcities, the crisis of the technetronic societies themselves seems to be a far more complex affair. In order to explain it, Brzezinski turns to Bell, who tells us how economic innovations create new occupational groups, new modes of thought, new types of interdependencies, and new esthetic perceptions, which in turn create a state of disequilibrium between social structure and political authority.[28] But Brzezinski also echoes Durkheim when he describes student violence as an escape from psychological strain, Marx when he invokes the boredom of functional specialization, and Ortega when he blames the troubles of America on the liberal passion for equality that in a technetronic age can no longer be "insulated by time and distance."[29] This eclecticism would not be intellectually debilitating per se. But Brzezinski makes little or no attempt to assign weight to individual factors, and this failure deprives his scheme of real explanatory power.

New Departures

While members of the academic establishment rushed to explain the political troubles of the Occident with reference to the system of production and to changes in levels of social complexity, most antiestablishment intellectuals fell back on classical Marxist categories, above all, on the category of scarcity. The explanations of the individual writers vary. Some stress the Marxist law of the declining rate of return; others point to the deleterious consequences of capitalist competition; yet others attribute the crisis of modern capitalism to the conflicting imperatives of mass consumerism and capital accumulation. But whatever their explanations, the leading members of this school—Louis Althusser, Nicos Poulantzas, Joachim Hirsch, and Claus Offe[30] —have all derived a new theory of the state from the condition of relative scarcity. This theory recognizes the relative "autonomy" of the state from economic classes and its emergence as a social force in its own right. Ever more pressed to regulate and to redistribute, the capitalist state becomes involved in hitherto "marginal fields (such as the training of labor power, town-planning, transport, health, environment)," as well as in the "reproduction and valorization of capital," and, ultimately, in the regulation of consumption.[31] The extent of this involvement is evident from the "considerably enhanced role of the indirect wage (measured by the quantity and price of collective means of consumption and of social benefits) in comparison to the direct wage."[32] The result is the "irresistible rise of the state administration,"[33] and the decline of the traditional institutions of liberal democracy.

Most of these theories represent little more than the use of Marxist terminology to describe the political effects of Keynesianism. They could well have been written by any conservative critic of the welfare state bemoaning the rise of bureaucratic authoritarianism, except that the Marxist writers move quickly to put the modern capitalist state in a larger global context. Their line of reasoning may be summarized under four points: (1) in order to maintain social peace, the elites of the core countries are under steady pressure to increase levels of mass consumption; (2) short of diminishing the capitalists' rate of return, the high living standards of the industrial nations can only be maintained by expropriating the surplus of backward nations; (3) however, given the rising consciousness of the masses of the peripheral nations, expropriation requires ever increasing levels of military expenditure and involvement; (4) as these expenditures increase, the costs of enforcement tend to vitiate their material benefits. In short, the recent troubles of the advanced industrial societies reflect the more profound contradictions of contemporary capitalism and imperialism.[34]

Yet another, and a somewhat less concisely formulated, theory shares the Marxist emphasis on scarcity but does not subscribe to the dialectics of the Marxist argument. The central variable of the theory is the obsolescence of technologies: the rise and the decline of global economic centers are explained by the "exploitation and subsequent exhaustion of major technological breakthroughs,"[35] which in turn are described as the "primary determinants" of labor productivity, investment activity, and the prevailing pattern of international division of labor. More specifically, the theory holds that the useful lifespan of technologies is finite. Societies innovate, then adapt their social institutions and material expectations to the new technology, but in time, the very adaptations become the source of inertia for the economy. In this vein Carlo Cipolla explains the economic decline of Italy and the shift of the center of the European economy to the northwest triangle of the Continent in the seventeenth century. The very success of Italian manufacturers in an earlier age permitted the rise of a wage structure, production strategies, and entrepreneurial complacency, which at a later date prevented them from responding creatively to the rise of new mass markets for cheap linens and textiles. Thus while new opportunities presented themselves, "Italian manufacturers persisted in producing by traditional methods excellent, but outmoded, products,"[36] and in the process lost their economic primacy to the Dutch and the English.

Other authors seem to discern the same cycle of technological innovation and decay in the context of the modern world economy. Among them, Robert Gilpin, in an incisive study, relates the rise of Great Britain to a "cluster of breakthroughs" in the steam-powered manufacture of textiles and iron; the rise of Germany to the "systematic application of science to industrial production"; and the rise of the United States to a "cluster of innovations in managerial know-how" and advanced technologies in the electrical, petrochemical, and automotive industries.[37] In each of these instances, decline set in as a result of a slavish clinging to a once-successful mode of production. Once the threshold is passed, the flight of capital begins, and labor productivity begins to decline, but high consumer expectations and wages persist. The overload of demand and inertia then combine to produce a downward spiral of economic and political decay.

While these theories portray the process of economic decline quite adequately, they leave some doubt in our minds as to the final causes of the process. Phrases like the "first" or "second industrial revolution," we should remember, are convenient metaphors. Beneath them lurks neither a single dramatic breakthrough nor a neat cluster of events, but a long series of successful innovations and adaptations that in each of the above-cited historical instances covered the span of at least a century. During these long spans of time, the core economies faced, not one, but numerous challenges, successful response to which required creativity and a great deal of social discipline. The question is, if it could be done once, twice, or ninety-nine times, why not the hundredth time? Is it possible that in formulating the proposition we have become the victims of circular reasoning? It is true that inertia slows down innovation, but it is also true that innovation means finding the ways of overcoming institutional inertia.

Then there is the nexus between economic decline and political instability. Normally—that is, within the conventional paradigms of political economy—we are inclined to put economics before politics: it is the new scarcity that shatters the stability of old authority. But such is not always the case, certainly not in the contemporary political crises of advanced industrial capitalism. Indeed, there is much in the evidence to suggest that the very opposite was the case. Here political turmoil and crisis surface and then peak not in times of economic depression, but in times of unprecedented material prosperity. This is evident not only from standard statistical sources but also from the writings of many social critics, including radicals, who alternately extolled or bemoaned this prosperity and even put forth the hypothesis that Western societies had reached the "post-scarcity" stage.[38] Appropriately, the prophet of this radicalism was not the mature Marx with his theories of immiseration, but the young Marx with his middle-class preoccupation with alienation and ennui. And as another, more recent, writer noted, this was not so much a revolt of masses suffering from the lack of amenities as of elites suffering from a scarcity of meanings.[39] The archetypal revolutionary of the 1960's was the offspring of the educated upper classes, demanding to know "what had gone wrong" and facing high government officials who readily admitted that they did not have the answer. To put it differently, this was a cultural crisis with grave implications for politics. The economic troubles of the 1970's and 1980's followed this cultural crisis and may well have been created by it.

A crisis of culture emancipated from the tensions of the social and economic structure does not fit easily into the conventional paradigm of sociology. But signs of the existence of just such a crisis were abundant and created one more of those "puzzles" that the old paradigm could not handle. Bit by bit, awareness of this anomaly spread and became evident even in the writings of some of the erstwhile post-industrialists. Thus although Bell's analysis of post-industrial society pivots around the notion of technological progress, in examining the ramifications of social change further, he is led to observe that "culture . . . in contemporary western society has achieved considerable autonomy," so that "at times" it may be treated as an "independent variable," capable of explaining social change.[40] This formula appears as an afterthought, proposed in an almost offhanded manner, but it is spelled out more clearly in Bell's next volume of essays on *The Cultural Contradictions of Capitalism*. In it Bell moves a long way from the technological reductionism of his earlier work and rejects the classical notion "that changes in the social structure determine man's imaginative reach."[41] Here, the dependent variable is the cohesion, or "fabric" of society, which Bell relates to the level of harmony or "discordance" among three autonomous social realms: the techno-economic, the political, and the cultural. These, he explains, "are not congruent with each other, and have different rhythms of change; they follow different norms, which legitimate different, and even contrasting, patterns of behavior."[42] Thus while technology is linear and inherently progressive, in culture "there is always *ricorso*, a return to the concerns and questions that are existential agonies of human beings."[43] And *ricorso* in culture will produce *Dekadenz*, permeating not only the arts, but politics and economics as well.

Still more interesting than this liberal departure from the classical paradigm is the incipient rebellion of a group of Marxist writers against the rigidities of classical sociological schemes. These writers recognize the role of the economic base as a "determinant in the last instance."[44] But, inspired by the recently unearthed and translated writings of Antonio Gramsci (1891–1937),[45] they also assign the state a new role in shaping mass consciousness through its ideological state apparatus (or ISA), argue that hegemony (read "authority") is a matter of ideology, and hold that elites rule by virtue not only of their control over the means of production but also of their ability to create ideas. Overall, political hegemony and social cohesion are the functions of two processes: the ability of society to produce goods and services; and the ability of elites to reproduce society as a legitimate entity. And if the production of goods and services may be easily reduced to objective conditions, the elite's reproduction of society may well become a matter of "extreme energy, decisiveness, resolution, and fanatical belief."[46] If so, we are only a step away from recognizing that cultural and ideological crises can occur independently from crises of the economic base.

These themes are echoed and further developed by Jürgen Habermas, whose voluminous writings aim at nothing less than a synthesis between the works of Marx and Weber, or, more immediately, of Marx and Talcott Parsons. Like other radical intellectuals of his generation, Habermas is explicitly critical of the "enlightenment paradigm" (derived from Newtonian physics), and of the classical idea that advances in technology and science are accompanied by moral and political improvements.[47] The reasons for his disappointment are not hard to discern. They stem from the inadequacies of the classical paradigm in providing explanations for the political problems of the advanced industrial countries of the West, where

in the last twenty years or so conflicts have developed . . . that in many respects deviate from the pattern of institutionalized conflict over redistribution in the welfare state. These [conflicts] no longer flare up in the domain of material reproduction; they are not channeled through parties and associations. . . . Rather, these new conflicts arise in the domains of cultural reproduction, social integration, and socialization; they are expressed by subinstitutional, and, at any rate extraparliamentary, forms of protest. . . . They do not primarily concern problems of compensation that the welfare state can provide, but the issue of protecting endangered . . . ways of life. In short, the new conflicts are sparked not by problems of redistribution, but by issues concerning the grammar of forms of life [*Grammatik der Lebensformen*].[48]

In order to deal with these conflicts, Habermas, like Parsons, distinguishes between the social and the cultural system, (or, in his own idiom, between "system" and "lifeworld"). Also, much like Parsons in his later works, Habermas shifts our attention from consciousness to symbolic systems on which meanings, and hence the effective pursuit of human objectives, rest. Rational action thus derives from "illocutionary acts by virtue of their internal connection with reasons, and the corresponding possibility of intersubjective recognition based on insight rather than external force."[49] These are bold ideas reflecting Habermas's desire "to appropriate" Weber and Parsons for progressive social thinking, but when all is said and done, and when the readers finally work their ways through these heavy tomes, some questions remain as to whether this appropriation is indeed, as Habermas claims, "in the spirit of western Marxism."[50]

Revolutionary as these formulations may be from the perspective of liberal and Marxist sociology, they can easily be accommodated within the conservative sociological paradigm associated with the names of Vilfredo Pareto (1848–1923) and

Gaetano Mosca (1858–1941).[51] Largely shunned by the dominant currents of academic inquiry, the works of these writers
focus our attention on qualities of leadership, which they identify with the ability of elites to create intellectual constructs—
rationalizations (Pareto) or formulae and myths (Mosca)—or
to their ability to make sense of them by exemplary or heroic
behavior. As long as elites possess this ability, they will be able
to strike out boldly, to adapt and innovate, and to exercise effective control over the societies they lead. Mass discontent,
fueled by scarcities and deprivation, may give rise to revolutionary movements, but revolutions will be successful only if
and when the old elites have lost direction and purpose, when
the symbols they have created no longer make sense even to
themselves. This piece of wisdom was shared by a number of
Marxist writers, among them Lenin and Trotsky, and probably
influenced the more recent revisionism of Gramsci and Althusser, even though it runs counter to the fundamental tenets
of historical materialism (for it is not easy to explain how the
consciousness of an elite can survive the disintegration of
structures whose very existence it presumably reflects). But
whether or not this concept of the revolutionary situation is
compatible with classical Marxism, Pareto and Mosca carry the
proposition one step further, arguing that a revolutionary situation or fundamental change in the political order can come
about even in the absence of mass discontent, solely as a result
of a declining sense of duty and purpose among the elites.
When their sense of duty and purpose are on the wane, elites
can no longer set examples to others, nor can they act in a coherent way. Society then begins to drift, and the diffidence of
the elite will soon be manifest, not only in political decay, but
also in the slackening of economic enterprise, artistic expression, and intellectual curiosity.

The concept of culture as an independent variable is still
more clearly articulated in the once-famous work of Oswald
Spengler (1880–1936), *The Decline of the West*.[52] The master concept of this work is *Kultur*, defined as a network of ideas and

symbols that serve as links among individuals and, not unlike Durkheim's "culture," influence their behavior. Because of these symbolic systems amorphous masses of people turn into "living and flowing currents of history,"[53] following a definite life cycle, much like Pareto's elite. There are traces here of Spencer's functionalism, for "politics is the way in which this fluent being maintains itself."[54] There are likewise faint echoes of Nietzsche's will to power. But the emphasis is on the cognitive, on the role of ideas. "Culture," writes Spengler, "possesses its own systemic psychology, just as it possesses its own style and knowledge of man,"[55] and changes in this style will be reflected in all other realms of social existence: in politics, economics, the arts, science, architecture, philosophy, and mathematics. When cultures peak, they all peak in a similar fashion, acquiring identical forms of expression that make intercultural comparisons both possible and intellectually worthwhile. The major threshold in the life cycle is between culture and civilization, the latter being simply culture in decline. It implies a shift from a practical-minded, collectivity-oriented, philosophical absolutism to the sensuous, self-oriented relativism that is the quintessence of decadence.

A Theory of Culture?

But why do cultures "exhaust" themselves? Why do elites "lose their will," or go into decline even in the absence of compelling necessities? Why do revolutions occur at a time of material abundance and technological progress? Answers to these questions are few and far between. Though Pareto and Mosca give us a vivid description of the process of decay, juxtaposing the behavior of elites on the rise and in decline, for the most part they do not address the problem of causality. Or if and when they do, they leave us with tautologies and platitudes: elites decline because they are no longer capable of ruthlessness or because they have lost the foresight to co-opt potential competitors from the lower classes. In a like manner,

Spengler's *Untergang* provides us with a vibrant description of how civilizations pass from their "practical, far-seeing, outward-directed" Faustian phase ("whose symbol is pure and limitless space") to sensuous Apollonian decadence. Spengler includes his captivating analysis of how culture "possesses its own systematic psychology," with all its own peculiar expressions in economics, politics, and intellectual life. But when it comes to identifying the *causa causans*, or the demiurge of the historical cycle, Spengler is as disappointing as his Italian colleagues, for he offers nothing but the tired biological analogy of aging that turns his empiricism into mysticism. Nor are the modern-day Paretans of the Left more illuminating. For while they have come to realize that culture is not a fixed quantity but must be reproduced by elites day by day, they fail to tell us when and why elites may lose their "communicative competence" (Habermas), or ability to regenerate the sources of their legitimacy.

Nevertheless, we may go just one step further by introducing into our discussion some elements of contemporary social psychology and cultural anthropology. In essence, these elements tell us that culture is not virtue, will, or normative injunction, but a "cognitive map,"[56] a symbolic instrument of *Verstehen*, or understanding, for the chaotic signals of the external world. It is in this vein that Habermas speaks of "encoded representations of social reproduction,"[57] echoing Parsons, who regards human action as "cultural" when "meanings and intentions are framed in terms of symbolic systems (including codes through which they operate in patterns)," and suggests that culture "structures commitments vis-à-vis ultimate reality into meaningful orientations toward the social environment."[58] The term "cognitive map" is particularly expressive, since the function of maps is to orient travelers on unfamiliar terrain. If some of the symbols on the map fail to conform to reality, the whole map may lose credibility.

In more than one way, these cognitive maps are like Kuhn's scientific paradigms. They are the products of deliberate effort, and their function is to organize facts, events, and discoveries that come society's way. As long as these bits of information can be accommodated within the accepted cultural matrix, the actors will be able to pursue their interests and to respond creatively and innovatively to the challenges they face. In other words, "normal society," like "normal science," presupposes a coherent, instrumental framework of symbols, accepted by the bulk of the community.[59] A condition of dissonance arises when new facts appear, but cannot be accommodated within the existing paradigm, or cognitive map. When this occurs, elites, societies, and civilizations will lose their capacity to act on their self-interest in a coherent and meaningful way. The stage is then set for cultural crisis and social change.

Like the older Weberian epistemology, these theories of cognitive consistency and dissonance have an essentially rationalistic view of human affairs. There is room in them for incoherence and disjuncture between ends and means. But incoherence here is a matter, not of "passion," but of incomprehension, the lack of ability to assess all the variables that bear on a particular outcome. Resting on this fundamental premise, contemporary cultural paradigms rescue rationality at the expense of certainty. For in them culture may unravel not only as a result of cumulative social change, but under the impact of a "single act," or event, that does not fit into the accepted intellectual matrix. Such an act, or event, can reveal the emptiness of sacred beliefs and "tear society to shreds," "provided that it is so absurd as to be incomprehensible," or has "the shocking senselessness of gratuitous blasphemy."[60] These are the words of one of Joseph Conrad's heroes, quoted by Daniel Bell to make a general point about the fragility of society and civilization. And in doing so, he carries Weber's idea to its logical conclusion: if the prophet and the hero can create and validate cultures, the antihero and the antiprophet can likewise destroy them by purposeful behavior. Societies, by this reasoning, can not only die of old age, but also succumb to heart attack. True, the antiheroic deed may not destroy society in a "flash" as Conrad's terrorist believed.[61] But the trauma of an act of profaning sacred assumptions may raise grave doubts about society's proclaimed worth and more noble qualities. If Lee Harvey Oswald's bullet did not destroy American society, it certainly did more to undermine its "integration" than all the microchips and technetronic devices of the decade.

This proposition, of course, is likely to be controversial. To some practitioners of social science, the proposition that a culture or a society may be fragmented by a single daring act or traumatic event may appear to be the rankest form of voluntarism, and a proposition to this effect a calculated attempt to undermine the enterprise of theorizing about human affairs. They may regard it, in the words of one writer, as a regrettable display of "indifference to the overall pattern and ultimate character of history," and a failure to discern "determinate life cycles" in the history of societies and civilizations.[62] Others, however, may be persuaded that this mode of thinking represents a strand of epistemological realism, a belated attempt to wean social science from its unconditional attachment to necessity, and another genuine intellectual breakthrough that can lead us to a nonteleological view of history and change.

Conclusions

Paradigm Shifts

Our journey is now coming to an end. In the course of it, we have examined the categories of the classical paradigm, the challenges that the discipline encountered, and the ways in which these challenges have been answered by social scientists. That the paradigm shifts are far from complete, that comparative politics, economics, and sociology are still in a state of ferment, is obvious from the previous pages. Yet, at the same time, the process has gone far enough to permit us to take stock and to pull together the different threads of theory around a few general principles.

In order to do so, we may have to return, if only briefly, to the categories of the classical paradigm as they evolved between the end of the eighteenth and the middle of the twentieth centuries. Central to this paradigm, as we will recall, is the concept of innovation—the institutionalization of technological innovations and scientific discoveries—in the quest for more effective mastery over our material environment. Whether in the writings of Smith, Marx, Spencer, Durkheim, Weber, or, later, Parsons, aspects of this process of innovation occupy an important position and permit us to formulate two general theories of political change.

The first of these two theories attempts to explain political behavior and has two critical components that act as intervening variables between innovation and political outcome. The one is motivational and refers to self-interest in optimizing one's position in society. This variable is intimately related to—and circumscribed by—social role. The other variable is cognitive. Appearing as consciousness with Marx, *sagesse* with Comte, and *Verstehen* with Weber, it refers to the ways in which people comprehend, structure, and define the situations in which they find themselves. When technological innovation occurs, so this theory tells us, there will be changes both in social roles (and interests) and in the systems of belief that allow actors to structure their behavior in the pursuit of gain. In this manner, classical theories of class may be linked with theories of "mobilization," rationalization, and "fundamental democratization."

The second theory is systemic, in the sense that it deals with society as a whole and rests on an equilibrium concept that was characteristic of social thinking in the Newtonian age. This theory aims to explain patterns, or systems, of authority and also has two main explanatory variables—complexity and scarcity. As technologies of production (transport, warfare) become more sophisticated, so the explanation runs, the division of labor in society will become more and more complex. Such complexity then requires and predicts more complex methods of coordination and control, and the functional specialization of government. In brief, this is a theory of bureaucratization. The form of government, however, is a function of available resources. When scarcity diminishes as a result of successful technological innovation, societies will be able to adapt to complexity without resorting to coercion and repressive instruments. Bureaucratization may thus be accompanied by pluralization and democracy. This, at any rate, was the experience of Britain and a few other societies of the Occident.

The intellectual developments of the past decade and the

rise of the new paradigm did not destroy the validity of these theories. They only undermined their claims to universality. Much like the Newtonian laws of physics, which remain valid at some velocities but not at others, these laws of classical sociology and economics remain relevant as explanations of the politics of the core, but not of the global peripheries. Nor does the new paradigm imply the discovery of a whole range of new categories. Rather, like Einstein's reconceptualization of the notions of time and space, the globalization of the systems concept provides a new way of looking at old categories.

In the first place, the globalization of the systems concept has affected the ways in which we now look at structure and interest. If beforehand sociology treated interest mainly as the function of one's position in the social hierarchy, now we have been led to realize that interest is also the function of one's position in a larger, global hierarchy. A ruling class is still a ruling class, and a proletariat is still a proletariat. But the motivations and dispositions of the elites of have-not nations will be different from those of the societies of global privilege, and the proletariat of privileged nations will have different forms of class consciousness than the lower classes of societies on the global peripheries. This circumstance, rather than various cultural hypotheses, may explain why the English working class in the nineteenth century and the American in the twentieth have been relatively complacent about inequalities in their own societies, and conversely, why the elites of such self-styled "proletarian nations" as Italy and Germany turned to political strategies that were conservative at home but radical in an international context.

As a corollary, the new paradigm has changed the parameters for the study of complexity and scarcity. As before, the paradigm points to the nexus between innovation and the division of labor, not in particular societies, but in the larger world system. To put it differently, the new paradigm does not tell us to study increasing differentiation within societies, but the increasing differentiation of the world between simple and complex societies. As in the old theory, political development and the rise of the modern state are responses to complexity, not only to social complexity, but to the complexities of the external environment as well. In the new theory, the frequent disjuncture between modern state and backward society is not a reversal of natural historical sequence, but the logical response of a simple society to its complex environment. Within the same parameters, scarcity and abundance become relative concepts, measured against the changing standards of core societies that can transform development into decay in the societies of the periphery. This, at least, is one of the ways in which we can speak of the "development of underdevelopment."

Just as the old paradigm did, so the new one recognizes the link between innovation and systems of belief. But whereas the old school tended to emphasize the causal nexus between innovation and *social* consciousness, the new paradigm reminds us forcefully that ideas are not confined by either political boundaries or developmental states. Rather, they float freely from society to society and from continent to continent. Social innovation, in other words, may result in changes of global consciousness. It may be responsible for changes in the whole stock of transnational knowledge and assumptions that are used to structure expectations and behavior. These changes will affect what in the old days used to be referred to as the *Zeitgeist*, a category near and dear to historians but alien to the classical sociologist. It is true though that as ideas move from core to periphery, they will encounter different configurations of interest, giving rise to different institutional responses and patterns of behavior. The ideas of modern secularism and popular sovereignty are cases in point. Whereas in the West they gave rise to parliamentary democracy, elsewhere the corresponding institutional expression is most frequently bureaucratic authoritarianism.

Structuralism and the Modern World System

The theories that emerged from the new paradigm are structural theories in the sense that they are based on contingency and see contingencies as creators of "confining conditions." In Siegfried Nagel's imaginative metaphor, such contingencies are best conceived of as forces creating a field of attraction around a magnetic core.[1] In the instance of world system theories, the contingency arises from the ongoing innovative experience of the West, which, whether on account of international competition, demonstration effects, or surplus transfer, exerts its force over classes and states and modifies their behavior in predictable ways.

The question that this mode of theorizing inevitably raises concerns the "hardness" of the structure and the ability of the theory to account for the deviant cases in which the actors managed to escape the force field, or broke through the confining conditions created by the initial contingency. Over the years, this question has been answered in one of two ways. To some theorists the field may appear to be of variable intensity, exerting different levels of force at different locations. To others, the field itself may appear to be constant, but the objects within it will have variable properties and propensities. In this conception of structure, confining conditions are like so many walls, not insurmountably high, but high enough to daunt all but the most adept athletes. Actors can accomplish breakthroughs on account of unique propensities.

This conception of structuralism inevitably takes us back to the variable of culture, to Smith's idea of "virtue," or still more profitably to Veblen's "cultural pedigree"[2] that latecomers must possess in order to catch up with those whom history has "thrown in the lead."[3] The difference between these two theories is important. For whereas Smith's classical formula tells us that "self-command" and "fellow feeling" are prerequisites of successful innovation, Veblen reminds us that "catching up" requires both more and different virtues than the pioneering experience. This should be borne in mind by both scholar and statesman. For generations now we have exhorted others to acquire Western ways, and to adopt our norms in order to succeed. Yet Veblen's formula tells us that such norms, or their functional equivalents, are not enough. What we need to formulate is not just a universal theory of virtue, but a kind of theory of "surplus virtue," as a requisite of breakthrough and successful late development.

At this point though, we should remind ourselves that the new paradigm and its structuralism have taken us far beyond the idea of developmental breakthroughs. The old paradigm, with its emphasis on the *social* system, tended to focus on internal solutions and remedies, above all, on the remedies of modernization and development. Under the reign of the old paradigm the underprivileged nations, much like the underprivileged classes of Victorian England in the nineteenth century, were assured that self-improvement was the way they could raise themselves to the level of the "better placed" nations of the international community. Meanwhile a quest for alternative solutions to their problems was dismissed as utopian and irrational.

The new sociology of the global division of labor has refocused our attention to a broader range of choices available to overcome the "confining conditions" of international inequality. The common denominator among these choices is that their immediate object is the *external*, rather than internal, environment. What the new paradigm suggests is that besides tinkering with the structures of their own society and economy, the elites of the peripheral nations may seek to reduce social strain by resorting to war or to revolutionary strategies designed to change the structure and operational principles of the larger world system. This they may do in quest for ultimate solutions or in search of incremental advantage, and even if they fall short of the former, they may accomplish the latter objective.

Culture, Structure, and the Limits of Theory

To repeat then, classical political sociology and economy experienced their first major crisis when social scientists attempted to use the old categories to explain politics in the non-Western world. This crisis was resolved by the new structuralism of the world system paradigm that shifted our attention from the social to the global division of labor. Meanwhile, a second intellectual crisis was triggered by a series of unanticipated developments in the advanced industrial countries proper. These events started the trend away from structural to cultural paradigms and explanations.

Although these two paradigm shifts seem to be moving in opposite directions, by no means do they represent contradictory developments. Indeed, far from being mutually exclusive, they are neatly complementary. Whereas the one is contingent on innovation, the other attempts to explain innovation not merely as a single historical event, but as an ongoing process that requires the steady reproduction of beliefs and symbolic systems. If the structural paradigm allows us to inquire into the consequences of continued Western success, the cultural paradigm encourages us to think about the prospects of cultural reproduction and disintegration. By pondering these prospects we can develop yet another grand scenario for the future of the modern world system, in which the identity of the core nations may change, but the structure of inequality remains.

The final question here is whether this cultural paradigm will allow us to formulate theories that can not only describe, but also predict, cultural change. In the more optimistic 1950's we would have answered this question quickly and affirmatively, proceeding to stake out our path "toward a general theory of culture change," perhaps by trying to identify weak and strong, or focal and peripheral, points in cultural systems. For good or bad, in the interim we have grown more cautious. Today we are ready to accept the idea of structures dependent on the constant reproduction of culture, but instead of formulating yet another general theory, we seem to be content with discerning loci of indeterminacy in larger cycles of change. In this way, to be sure, we skirt some of the weightiest philosophical problems inherent in the ideas of determinism and voluntarism, phenomenology and system building. Like the Hindu mythologists, so aptly quoted by Clifford Geertz,[4] we confidently describe the world as resting on a platform, held up by an elephant, which in turn is held up by a turtle. But then we shy away from asking questions as to what the turtle rests on.

As we ponder such questions, we are apt to relive some of the age-old dilemmas of science, captured by Archimedes's famous boast, in which he promised to create, or recreate, a universe, if he only could find a fixed point outside it. Not having found it, he resigned himself to the imperfections of his art, which was the art of theorizing. Like him, the social scientists create robust structures in the knowledge that they may be standing on quicksand. And still they go on, because this is the only way to create some order in disorder and to discern pattern, without denying the ultimate uncertainty that makes the study of human affairs so exasperating yet so tantalizing.

Notes

Notes

Introduction

1. Thomas S. Kuhn, *The Structure of Scientific Revolutions* (Chicago, 1962). (A second, substantially revised edition of the volume appeared in 1970; references in the text are to the original edition.) For a discussion of Kuhn's volume, see Gary Cutting, ed., *Paradigms and Revolutions* (Notre Dame, Ind., 1980), especially Douglas L. Eckberg and Lester Hill, "The Paradigm Concept and Sociology: A Critical Review," pp. 117–36; Sheldon Wolin, "Paradigms and Political Theories," pp. 160–94; and David Hollinger, "T. S. Kuhn's Theory of Science and Its Implications for History," pp. 195–222.

2. Kuhn, p. 10. The term became highly popular with social scientists, only to be changed by Kuhn to "disciplinary matrix" in the second edition of the volume. See Eckberg and Hill, in Cutting, p. 118.

3. Kuhn, pp. 10–13.

4. Ibid., p. 77.

5. Ibid., p. 91.

6. This enterprise may be contrary to Kuhn's original intentions, for he describes the social sciences as "pre-paradigmatic," that is, as unable to command disciplinary consensus. Over the years, however, the paradigm concept gained quick and widespread acceptance among students of social science and the humanities. See Eckberg and Hill, Wolin, and Hollinger in Cutting. For further references see Talcott Parsons, *Societies: Evolutionary and Comparative Perspectives* (Englewood Cliffs, N.J., 1966), p. 21; Albert O. Hirschman, *The Passions and the Interests* (Princeton, N.J., 1977), p. 42; also, Jeffrey C. Alex-

ander, *The Classical Attempt at Theoretical Synthesis* (Berkeley, Calif., 1983), p. xx.

7. For Pareto, Mosca, and Spengler, see Ch. 5, n. 51.

Chapter 1

1. Auguste Comte, *Cours de philosophie positive*, 2d ed., 4 vols. (Paris, 1864). For a summary of this work and for Comte's contributions to social science, see Randall Collins and Michael Makowsky, *The Discovery of Society* (New York, 1972), pp. 26–32.

2. See Lawrence Stone's amusing and revealing comment that "[during] the middle and late seventeenth century England [had] adumbrated or developed all the basic ideas of the Enlightenment: rationalism and religious toleration, a rejection of superstition and horror of enthusiasm, a disclaimer to any God-given mastery over nature, . . . contractual sovereignty and propertied democracy; empirical scientific investigation and Newtonian cosmology. Having accomplished all this, England left it to the French . . . to adapt and develop the ideas, invent the name Enlightenment, and to take the credit." Lawrence Stone, "The New Eighteenth Century," *New York Review of Books*, Mar. 29, 1984, p. 42.

3. Adam Smith, *Wealth of Nations*, with an Introduction by Andrew Skinner (New York, 1982).

4. William Robertson, *Collected Works* (1812), vol. 5, p. 128. Quoted by Andrew Skinner in the Introduction to Smith, *Wealth*, pp. 31, 88n.

5. Smith, *Wealth*, pp. 46, 109–15.

6. Ibid., p. 32.

7. Ibid., pp. 479–509.

8. Ibid., p. 30.

9. For this famous phrase, see Adam Smith, *Theory of Moral Sentiments* (London, 1853), p. 4.

10. Ibid., pp. 446–47; see also Smith, *Wealth*, p. 16.

11. Smith, *Wealth*, pp. 34–37.

12. It is sometimes overlooked that the qualities of "self-command" and "fellow feeling" point to two different sets of relationships. The former refers to habits and beliefs conducive to the effective marshaling of resources and is thus a precondition of effective development. The latter is required for, and so predicts, the effective functioning of a civic polity.

13. Karl Marx and Friedrich Engels, *The German Ideology*, in Robert C. Tucker, ed., *Marx-Engels Reader* (New York, 1972), pp. 115–27.

14. Karl Marx, *Capital*, 3 vols., Friedrich Engels, ed. (New York,

1975), vol. 1, chs. 25–32, esp. pp. 648–764. See also Marx and Engels, *Communist Manifesto*, in R. C. Tucker; and Marx, *Grundrisse der Kritik der politischen Oekonomie* (1857; rev. ed. 1859), in David McLellan, ed., *Karl Marx: Selected Writings* (London, 1977), pp. 348–87.

15. For this third point, see especially Marx's description of the various styles of the development of the consciousness of the proletariat within the capitalist system. Marx and Engels, *Communist Manifesto*, pp. 342–43.

16. See Karl Marx, "The Civil War in France," pp. 576–77, "The Eighteenth Brumaire," pp. 436–525, and "On Social Relations in Russia," pp. 589–99, in R. C. Tucker. In all three essays the question is whether the state is an instrument of social forces or is independent from them.

17. Karl Marx, "Wage Labour and Capital," in R. C. Tucker, p. 178.

18. Ibid., p. 185.

19. Ibid., p. 188.

20. Ibid.

21. Ibid., p. 180.

22. Ibid.

23. Herbert Spencer, *Principles of Sociology*, 6 vols. (London, 1876–97).

24. See "Advice to the Modernizers of Japan" (1892), in Herbert Spencer, *On Social Evolution*, J. D. Y. Peel, ed. (Chicago, 1972), pp. 253–57.

25. Spencer's thinking wavers between Lamarckian and Darwinian theory. The difference between the two is that in the former it is the organism, in the latter it is the species, that adapts to the challenges of the environment. In assuming that society adapts by differentiation, Spencer follows Lamarck. In describing the societies of the world as a species, of which the unfit will not reproduce themselves, Spencer follows in the footsteps of Darwin.

26. Spencer, *Social Evolution*, p. 138.

27. Ibid., p. 135.

28. Ibid., pp. 53–70, 134–41.

29. Ibid., p. 139.

30. Ibid., p. 67.

31. Ibid., p. xxxii.

32. Ibid., p. 171.

33. Ibid., p. 158.

34. Ibid., p. 154.

35. See Collins and Makowsky, p. 27.

36. F. S. Marvin, *Comte* (New York, 1964), p. 65.

37. Comte, *Cours de philosophie positive*, vol. 4, p. 425, as quoted in Steven Lukes, *Emile Durkheim* (New York, 1973), p. 141.

38. Comte, vol. 4, p. 428, in Lukes, p. 141.

39. Comte, vol. 4, p. 430, in Lukes, p. 142.

40. Ferdinand Tönnies, *Community and Society*, C. P. Loomis, trans. (New York, 1963), p. 65.

41. Ibid.

42. Emile Durkheim, *The Division of Labor in Society*, George Simpson, trans. (Glencoe, Ill., 1964), p. xix. Durkheim gives a more detailed discussion on pp. 233–56.

43. Above all ibid., pp. 111–32, but for a distinction between himself and Spencer, see pp. 200–206.

44. Ibid., p. 172.

45. Ibid.

46. Ibid.

47. Claude Lévi-Strauss, "Le totémisme aujourd'hui" (Paris, 1962), quoted in Lukes, p. 236n.

48. Claude Lévi-Strauss, "French Sociology," in George Gurvitch and Wilbert E. Moore, eds., *Twentieth Century Sociology* (New York, 1945), p. 518.

49. Max Weber, *The Sociology of Religion*, 4th rev. ed., E. Fischoff, trans., with an Introduction by Talcott Parsons (Boston, 1964), p. xxiii.

50. Max Weber, *The Theory of Social and Economic Organization*, A. M. Henderson and Talcott Parsons, trans. (Glencoe, Ill., 1964), p. 328.

51. Weber, *Sociology of Religion*, p. 59.

52. For a discussion of the concept of rationalization, see Weber, *Theory*, pp. 158–319, with Parsons's comments, pp. 78–87. A still more complete version is in Max Weber, *Economy and Society*, Guenther Roth and Claus Wittich, eds. (Berkeley, Calif., 1978), pp. 63–212.

53. Weber, *Theory*, pp. 184–90.

54. Ibid., pp. 181–84.

55. Weber, *Sociology of Religion*, pp. 32–46.

56. Max Weber, *The Protestant Ethic and the Spirit of Capitalism*, Talcott Parsons, trans. (New York, 1958), p. 181.

57. Ibid., p. 176.   58. Ibid., p. 182.

59. Ibid., pp. 182–83.   60. Weber, *Theory*, p. 327.

Chapter 2

1. Thorstein Veblen, *Imperial Germany and the Industrial Revolution*, 3d ed. (New York, 1954), p. 38. (First published 1915.)

2. Ibid., p. 39.   3. Ibid., p. 121.

4. Ibid., p. 129.   5. Ibid., p. 130.

6. Ibid., p. 132.   7. Ibid., p. 163.
8. Ibid.   9. Ibid., p. 261.
10. Vladimir I. Lenin, "Two Tactics of Social Democracy in the Democratic Revolution," in Lenin, *Selected Works* (Moscow, 1970), vol. 1, pp. 479–86.

11. G. V. Plekhanov, "On the Agrarian Question in Russia," quoted in Karl F. Wittfogel, *Oriental Despotism* (New Haven, Conn., 1957), pp. 390–91.

12. "Results and Prospects" (1906), in Leon Trotsky, *The Permanent Revolution and Results and Prospects*, with an Introduction by Peter Camejo (New York, 1969), p. 107.

13. Leon Trotsky, "Permanent Revolution," in ibid., p. 133.

14. Vladimir I. Lenin, "Imperialism, the Highest Stage of Capitalism," in Lenin, *Selected Works*, vol. 1., pp. 667–768.

15. Iosif V. Stalin, "The Foundations of Leninism," in H. Bruce Franklin, ed., *The Essential Stalin* (Garden City, N.Y., 1972), p. 90.

16. Ibid., p. 110.

17. Arthur Bentley, *The Process of Government* (Evanston, Ill., 1908), pp. 29, 259.

18. James H. Meisel, ed., *Pareto and Mosca* (Englewood Cliffs, N.J., 1965), p. 18; for the major works of Pareto and Mosca, see Ch. 5, n. 51.

19. Jeffrey C. Alexander, *The Modern Reconstruction of Classical Thought: Talcott Parsons* (Berkeley, Calif., 1983), p. 45.

20. Talcott Parsons, "The Present Position and Prospects of Systematic Theory in Sociology," in Parsons, *Essays in Sociological Theory*, rev. ed. (Glencoe, Ill., 1954), pp. 214–15.

21. Talcott Parsons, *Societies: Evolutionary and Comparative Perspectives* (Englewood Cliffs, N.J., 1966), p. 9.

22. Talcott Parsons and Edward A. Shils, eds., *Toward a General Theory of Action*, 2d ed. (New York, 1962), p. 7. (First published 1951.)

23. Ibid.   24. Ibid.
25. Ibid., p. 28.   26. Ibid., p. 17.

27. See Parsons's references to Roman Jakobson and Morris Halle, *Fundamentals of Language* (The Hague, 1956), and Noam Chomsky, *Syntactic Structures* (The Hague, 1957), in *Societies*, p. 20.

28. In Parsons's words, cultural tradition is "both . . . an object of orientation, and . . . an element in the orientation of action." Parsons and Shils, p. 7.

29. Ibid.

30. Parsons, *Societies*, p. 23.

31. See *Societies*, pp. 22–23, and Parsons and Shils, pp. 76–81.
32. Parsons and Shils, p. 81.
33. Ibid.
34. Parsons, *The Social System* (Glencoe, Ill., 1951), p. 449.
35. Parsons and Shils, pp. 78, 79.
36. Ibid., p. 78.
37. Ibid., pp. 78, 79.
38. Daniel Lerner, *The Passing of Traditional Society* (Glencoe, Ill., 1958), p. 438; quoted in part in Samuel P. Huntington, *Political Order in Changing Societies* (New Haven, Conn., 1968), p. 32.
39. For a comprehensive bibliography of the Parsonians, see Alexander, *Talcott Parsons*, pp. 319–21.
40. Marion J. Levy Jr., *The Family Revolution in Modern China* (Cambridge, Mass., 1949), *The Structure of Society* (Princeton, N.J., 1952), and *Modernization and the Structure of Societies* (Princeton, N.J., 1966).
41. Levy, *Structure of Society*, p. 149.
42. Levy defines function as "a condition, or state of affairs, resultant from the operation or mere persistence of a structure through time." Functional requisites in turn are defined as "minimum requirements that must 'preexist' for a unit of a given type in its setting to come into being or to change in particular ways." See ibid., pp. 56, 71.
43. Ibid., p. 151.
44. Ibid., pp. 149–98.
45. In Levy, *Modernization*.
46. Neil J. Smelser, *Social Change in the Industrial Revolution* (Chicago, 1959).
47. Ibid., p. 2.
48. Fred W. Riggs, *Administration in Developing Countries* (Boston, 1964).

49. Ibid., pp. 25–27.	50. Ibid., p. 463.
51. Ibid., p. 27.	52. Ibid., p. 110.
53. Ibid., p. 167.	54. Ibid., p. 113.
55. Ibid., p. 36.	56. Lerner, *Passing*, p. 45.
57. Ibid., p. 46.	58. Ibid., p. 49.
59. Ibid., p. 160.	60. Ibid., p. 399.

61. Karl W. Deutsch, "Social Mobilization and Political Development," *American Political Science Review*, 55, no. 3 (Sept. 1961): 493–502. Alex Inkeles and David H. Smith, *Becoming Modern: Individual Change in Six Developing Countries* (Cambridge, Mass., 1974).
62. See Karl Mannheim, *Man and Society in an Age of Reconstruction* (London, 1940), pp. 44, 53.

63. Gabriel A. Almond and James S. Coleman, *The Politics of the Developing Areas* (Princeton, N.J., 1960), p. 5.

64. See ibid., pp. 26–57.

65. Ibid., pp. 11, 24–26.

66. Gabriel A. Almond and G. Bingham Powell, *Comparative Politics: System, Process and Policy* (Boston, 1978), p. 25.

67. Ibid.

68. David A. Apter, *The Politics of Modernization* (Chicago, 1965), p. 43.

69. Ibid., p. 44.   70. Ibid., p. 67.

71. Ibid.   72. Ibid., p. 426.

73. Ibid.

74. Seymour M. Lipset, *Political Man* (Garden City, N.Y., 1960).

75. Ibid., p. 48.

76. Ibid., pp. 51–52.

77. Ibid., p. 54.

78. Walt W. Rostow, *The Stages of Economic Growth* (Cambridge, Eng., 1960), esp. pp. 1–16.

79. Cyril E. Black, *The Dynamics of Modernization: A Study in Comparative History* (New York, 1966), pp. 67–68.

80. Ibid., pp. 90–94.

81. Ibid., pp. 83–84.

82. Samuel P. Huntington, "The Change to Change: Modernization, Development and Politics," in Ray C. Macridis and Bernard E. Brown, eds., *Comparative Politics*, 4th ed. (Homewood, Ill., 1972), p. 409.

83. Talcott Parsons, "Some Sociological Aspects of Fascist Movements" (1945). Quoted in Alexander, *Talcott Parsons*, p. 65.

84. Isaac Deutscher, *Stalin* (New York, 1960).

85. Karl deSchweinitz, *Industrialization and Democracy* (New York, 1964); Robert L. Heilbroner, *The Great Ascent: The Struggle for Economic Development in Our Time* (New York, 1963); Alexander Gerschenkron, *Economic Backwardness in Historical Perspective* (Cambridge, Mass., 1962), pp. 1–30; David A. Apter, "System, Process and the Politics of Development," in Bert Hoselitz and Wilbert Moore, eds., *Industrialization and Society* (The Hague, 1963), pp. 135–59.

86. Reprinted in the volume of the same title.

87. Lerner, *Passing*, p. 45.

88. Lucian W. Pye, *Aspects of Political Development* (Boston, 1966), pp. 31–70.

89. Barrington Moore Jr., *The Social Origins of Dictatorship and Democracy* (Boston, 1966).

90. See R. H. Tawney, *The Agrarian Problem in the Sixteenth Century* (Evanston, Ill., 1967; first published 1912).

91. Reinhard Bendix, *Nation-Building and Citizenship* (New York, 1964).

92. Bendix, "Tradition and Modernity Reconsidered," *Comparative Studies in Society and History*, 9 (Apr. 1967): 292–346; republished in *Nation-Building and Citizenship*, 2d ed. (Berkeley, Calif., 1974), pp. 361–434. The following notes refer to the latter edition.

93. Ibid., pp. 387, 406.

94. Ibid., p. 408.

95. Ibid., p. 410.

96. Huntington, *Political Order*, p. 1.

97. See, for example, Huntington, "The Change to Change," p. 419. Perhaps the most effective criticism is by Charles Tilly in "Does Modernization Breed Revolution?" *Comparative Politics*, 5 (Apr. 1973): 429–47.

98. Huntington, *Political Order*, pp. 192–98.

Chapter 3

1. See Fred W. Riggs, *Administration in Developing Countries* (Boston, 1964), p. 38.

2. John H. Kautsky, *The Political Consequences of Modernization* (New York, 1972), p. 44.

3. See the discussion (Ch. 2, pp. 62–63) on Bendix; also his "Tradition and Modernity Reconsidered," *Comparative Studies in Society and History*, 9 (Apr. 1967): 292–346.

4. David A. Apter, *The Politics of Modernization* (Chicago, 1965), p. x.

5. Stanislaw Andreski, *Social Sciences as Sorcery* (New York, 1973), esp. pp. 59–93.

6. Barrington Moore Jr., "The New Scholasticism and the Study of Politics," in Moore, *Political Power and Social Theory* (New York, 1962), pp. 89–110.

7. James N. Rosenau, ed., *Linkage Politics: Essays on the Convergence of National and International Systems* (New York, 1969). Also Bendix, "Tradition and Modernity."

8. For the origins and "parentage" of the new paradigm, see J. Samuel Valenzuela and Arturo Valenzuela, "Modernization and Dependency: Alternative Perspectives in the Study of Latin American Underdevelopment," in Heraldo Muñoz, ed., *From Dependency to Development* (Boulder, Colo., 1981), pp. 35–41.

9. For a good representative sample of this literature, see the following two collections: K. T. Fann and Donald C. Hodges, eds., *Readings in U.S. Imperialism* (Boston, 1971); and James D. Cockcroft, André Gunder Frank, and Dale Johnson, eds., *Dependence and Underdevelopment* (New York, 1972). Also Valenzuela and Valenzuela, pp. 15–43.

10. André Gunder Frank, *Capitalism and Underdevelopment in Latin America* (New York, 1967), p. 9.

11. Harry Magdoff, *The Age of Imperialism* (New York, 1966), p. 16.

12. See Dale Johnson, "Dependence and the International System," in Cockcroft, Frank, and Johnson, pp. 100–102; for another typology, see Theotonio Dos Santos, "The Structure of Dependence," in Fann and Hodges, pp. 225–36, esp. p. 227.

13. Susanne Bodenheimer, "Dependency and Imperialism: The Roots of Latin American Underdevelopment," in Fann and Hodges, pp. 163–64.

14. For a good summary of the radical argument see Harry Magdoff and Paul Sweezy, "Notes on the Multinational Corporation," in Fann and Hodges, pp. 93–115. For a more conventional view, with an extensive bibliography, see Robert Gilpin, *U.S. Power and the Multinational Corporation* (New York, 1975). For a sympathetic view, see Business Week Team, *The Decline of U.S. Power* (Boston, 1980), esp. pp. 158–69. For the evolution of the study of multinational corporations and its place within theories of dependency and imperialism, see Peter Evans, *Dependent Development: The Alliance of Multinational, State and Local Capital in Brazil* (Princeton, N.J., 1979), esp. pp. 3–54.

15. See, in Fann and Hodges, James O'Connor, "The Meaning of Economic Imperialism," pp. 23–68, Theotonio Dos Santos, "The Structure of Dependence," pp. 225–36, and André Gunder Frank, "On the Mechanisms of Imperialism," pp. 237–48. Also Samir Amin, *Accumulation on a World Scale: A Critique of the Theory of Underdevelopment*, Brian Price, trans. (New York, 1974).

16. See Marx, *Capital*, Friedrich Engels, ed. (New York, 1975), vol. 1, pp. 312–418, 508–26; and "Wage Labour and Capital," in Robert C. Tucker, *Marx-Engels Reader* (New York, 1972), pp. 167–90.

17. Immanuel Wallerstein, *The Modern World System* (New York, 1974), p. 302.

18. See Robert Brenner, "The Origins of Capitalist Development: A Critique of Neo-Smithian Marxism," *New Left Review*, 104 (July–Aug. 1977): 25–93.

19. Wallerstein, p. 348.   20. Ibid., pp. 196, 191.

21. Ibid., p. 309.   22. Ibid., p. 99.

23. Arghiri Emmanuel, *Unequal Exchange: Study of the Imperialism of Trade* (New York, 1972).

24. See Charles Bettelheim's remarks in Appendix I to Emmanuel, esp. pp. 314–15.

25. See Michael J. Piore, "The Technological Foundations of Dualism and Discontinuity," in Suzanne Berger and Michael J. Piore, eds., *Dualism and Discontinuity in Industrial Societies* (Cambridge, Eng., 1980), pp. 53–83.

26. As noted, this theory is primarily associated with Raul Prebisch and the U.N. Commission for Latin American Economic Progress (CEPAL). See Raul Prebisch, *The Economic Development of Latin America and Its Problems* (New York, 1950); CEPAL, *The Economic Development of Latin America in the Postwar Period* (New York, 1964); and CEPAL, *External Financing in Latin America* (New York, 1965). For the CEPAL paradigm and a discussion of some of Prebisch's work, Albert O. Hirschman, "Ideologies of Economic Development in Latin America," in Hirschman, ed., *Latin American Issues: Essays and Comments* (New York, 1961), pp. 3–36, esp. pp. 14–16. For a radical critique of the theory and of Prebisch's conclusions, André Gunder Frank, "The Growth and Decline of Import Substitution," *Economic Bulletin for Latin America*, 9 (Mar. 1964).

27. Perry Anderson, *Lineages of the Absolutist State* (London, 1974), and Theda Skocpol, *States and Social Revolutions* (Cambridge, Eng., 1979).

28. P. Anderson, p. 431.

29. Skocpol, p. 41.

30. According to my own calculations, in 1890 six countries of South and East Europe (Spain, Portugal, Serbia, Bulgaria, Russia, and Ottoman Turkey) had average per capita incomes that equalled an estimated 37.5 percent of the average of the per capita incomes of seven "advanced" industrial nations (U.K., U.S., Belgium, France, Germany, Switzerland, and Sweden). Meanwhile their combined per capita government expenditures equalled 82.4 percent of those of the most developed states of the period. In thirteen Latin American countries average per capita GNP equalled 25.0 percent of the GNP for the advanced nations, while the figure for their government expenditures was 52.2 percent and for military spending 62.5 percent of that of the advanced nations. Calculations are based on Arthur S. Banks and Robert B. Textor, eds., *Cross-Polity Time Series* (Cambridge, Mass., 1972), esp. pp. 99–137.

31. For some references to the IDE, see Karl deSchweinitz, *Industrialization and Democracy* (New York, 1964); George Blanksten,

"Transference of Social and Political Loyalties," in Bert Hoselitz and Wilbert Moore, eds., *Industrialization and Society* (New York, 1963), p. 184; Ithiel de Sola Pool, "Communication in the Process of Modernization and Technological Change," in Hoselitz and Moore, p. 291; Daniel Lerner, *The Passing of Traditional Society* (Glencoe, Ill., 1958), and "Toward a Communication Theory of Modernization," in Lucian Pye, ed., *Communication and Political Development* (Princeton, N.J., 1963), p. 106; Benjamin J. Cohen, *The Question of Imperialism* (New York, 1973), esp. p. 160; and Helio Jaguribe, *Economic and Political Development* (Cambridge, Mass., 1968), pp. 42–45. Most of these works, however, point to the IDE as a stimulus for economic development, without fully developing the interdependent character of the relationship or the more complex consequences of relative scarcity for social mobility and political decay in peripheral societies. A significant step in examining these issues was made in Reinhard Bendix, *Kings and People* (Berkeley, Calif., 1979).

32. Reinhard Bendix, *Max Weber: An Intellectual Portrait* (Garden City, N.Y., 1962), p. 32.

33. Marx, "Wage Labour and Capital," p. 180.

34. Thorstein Veblen, *Imperial Germany and the Industrial Revolution*, 3d ed. (New York, 1954), p. 147. (First published 1915.)

35. Ibid., p. 208.

36. Ibid., p. 136.

37. R. B. Mitchell, ed., *European Historical Statistics, 1750–1850* (New York, 1975), pp. 427–29, 443–44.

38. Felix Colson, *De l'état present de Moldavie et de Valachie* (Paris, 1841), pp. 210–13.

39. Johann von Csaplovics, *Eine Gemälde von Ungarn* (Pest, 1829), vol. 1, p. 254.

40. Ruth Trouton, *Peasant Renaissance in Yugoslavia, 1900–1950* (London, 1952), pp. 71–72.

41. Claudio Véliz, *The Centralist Tradition in Latin America* (Princeton, N.J., 1980), pp. 168–72.

42. Charles W. Anderson, *Politics and Economic Change in Latin America* (Princeton, N.J., 1967), p. 22.

43. For these trade patterns see Banks and Textor, pp. 171–206.

44. For Serbia, Charles Jelavich, ed., *The Balkans in Transition* (Berkeley, Calif., 1960), p. 308; for Prussia, Weber in Bendix, *Max Weber*, p. 32; for Hungary, Andrew C. Janos, *The Politics of Backwardness in Hungary, 1825–1945* (Princeton, N.J., 1982), passim; for Romania, Stefan Zeletin, *Burghezia româna* (Bucharest, 1925); for Brazil, Jaguribe, p. 137; for Argentina, Véliz, p. 287.

45. Mihail Eminescu; see Andrew C. Janos, "Modernization and Decay in Historical Perspective: The Case of Romania," in Kenneth Jowitt, ed., *Social Change in Romania, 1860–1940* (Berkeley, Calif., U.C. Institute of International Studies Research Series, No. 36, 1978).

46. See Manfred Halpern, *The Politics of Social Change in the Middle East and North Africa* (Princeton, N.J., 1963), esp. pp. 51–78.

47. For the term, see Riggs, pp. 188–93. For a comparison between East Europe and contemporary "developing" countries, see Nicholas Spulber, *The State and Economic Development in Eastern Europe* (New York, 1966).

48. Constantin Dobrogeanu-Gherea, *Neo-iobagia* (Neo-serfdom) (Bucharest, 1912).

49. See Samuel P. Huntington, *Political Order in Changing Societies* (New Haven, Conn., 1968), pp. 39–78; or Karl Deutsch, "Social Mobilization and Political Development," *American Political Science Review*, 55, no. 3 (Sept. 1961): 493–502.

50. Statistics for fourteen European countries show that between 1910 and 1930 total enrollment at their universities oscillated between 0.06 and 0.125 percent of the entire population. See Desiré Laky, *Statistique des étudiants des universités en 1930* (Budapest, 1932), pp. 13–14.

51. Richard H. Holton, "Changing Demand and Consumption," in Wilbert E. Moore and Arnold S. Feldman, eds., *Labor Commitment and Social Change in Development Areas* (New York, 1950), pp. 210–16; or Mancur Olson Jr., "Rapid Growth as a De-Stabilizing Force," *Journal of Economic History*, 23 (Dec. 1963): 529–52. For a bibliography of other sources, see Ted R. Gurr, *Why Men Rebel* (Princeton, N.J., 1970), pp. 93–97, nn. 2–17.

52. See Gurr, pp. 98–99, nn. 19–24.

53. Anthony R. Oberschall, "Rising Expectations and Political Turmoil," *Journal of Development Studies*, 6 (Oct. 1969): 5–22.

54. Gurr, p. 100.   55. Oberschall, p. 10.
56. Ibid., p. 12.   57. Ibid., p. 15.
58. Ibid., pp. 7, 10. 59. Gurr, p. 93.
60. Ibid., p. 100.   61. Ibid., p. 101.

Chapter 4

1. J. P. Nettl and Ronald Robertson, *International Systems and the Modernization of Societies* (London, 1968), pp. 56–57.

2. In my opinion there are today five major competing models of Communist politics: (1) the ideological model, emphasizing the ar-

bitrariness of the system; (2) the Byzantine model, emphasizing cultural continuities in rituals and decision making; (3) the large-scale organizational model, in which habit and organizational complexity are seen to impose certain restraints on the actors; (4) the crypto-pluralist model that explains political outcomes in reference to group conflict in a noninstitutionalized setting; and (5) neo-Marxist models emphasizing class, quasi-proprietary relations, and "contradictions" between consumers and planners. For bibliographies on these approaches, see Daniel Bell, "Ten Theories in Search of Reality," in *The End of Ideology: On the Exhaustion of Political Ideas in the Fifties* (New York, 1961), pp. 315–54; Leonard J. Cohen and Jane O. Shapiro, eds., *Communist Systems in Comparative Perspective* (New York, 1974), pp. xix–xliv. For modern Marxist, or "post-Marxist," contributions in European "socialist societies," see Martin Carnoy, *The State and Political Theory* (Princeton, N.J., 1984), pp. 153–71. For individual contributions to the neo-Marxist models, see Charles Bettelheim, *Economic Calculation and Forms of Property* (New York, 1975); and Frank Parkin, *Class Inequality and Political Order* (New York, 1971).

3. Carl J. Friedrich and Zbigniew K. Brzezinski, *Totalitarian Dictatorship and Autocracy* (New York, 1956; a second, revised edition of the book was published in 1965 without Brzezinski's coauthorship); and Carl J. Friedrich, ed., *Totalitarianism* (Cambridge, Mass., 1954).

4. Hannah Arendt, *The Origins of Totalitarianism* (New York, 1951).

5. Ibid., pp. 305–40.

6. Norman Cohn, *The Pursuit of the Millennium* (New York, 1961), and J. L. Talmon, *The Origins of Totalitarian Democracy* (New York, 1951).

7. Arendt, "Epilogue" to the first Meridian edition of *The Origins of Totalitarianism* (New York, 1958), p. 485.

8. Arendt, *Totalitarianism* (New York, 1968), p. xvii.

9. See, as an example of the historical view, John Maynard, *The Russian Peasant and Other Studies* (London, 1947). For the "national psyche" view, see Geoffrey Gorer and John Rickman, *The People of Great Russia* (London, 1949). For the leadership view, see Nathan Leites, *A Study of Bolshevism* (Glencoe, Ill., 1954).

10. Edward Crankshaw, *Cracks in the Kremlin Wall* (New York, 1951).

11. Werner Philipp, quoted in Bell, "Ten Theories," p. 326 and p. 428, n. 108.

12. See Richard Pipes, ed., *Soviet Strategy in Europe* (New York, 1976).

13. Especially Barrington Moore Jr., *Terror and Progress, U.S.S.R.:*

Some Sources of Change and Stability in the Soviet Dictatorship (Cambridge, Mass., 1954; 2d ed. 1966); his earlier and equally impressive study, *Soviet Politics: The Dilemma of Power* (New York, 1950), deals with changes from Leninism to Stalinism in a similar vein, pointing to seemingly inevitable confrontations between ideology and social reality and to a process of adaptation to hard realities by postponing and "ritualizing" some elements of the ideology.

14. Samuel P. Huntington and Clement H. Moore, eds., *Authoritarian Politics in Modern Society: The Dynamics of Established One-Party Systems* (New York, 1970). See especially Huntington, "Social and Institutional Dynamics of One-Party Systems," pp. 3–47.

15. Ibid., p. 7. 16. Ibid., p. 23.

17. Ibid., p. 32. 18. Ibid.

19. Leon Trotsky, *The Revolution Betrayed*, 4th ed. (New York, 1970).

20. Milovan Djilas, *The New Class: An Analysis of the Communist System* (New York, 1962).

21. Among them, W. B. Bland, *The Restoration of Capitalism in the Soviet Union* (Wembly, Eng., 1980); Tony Cliff, *State Capitalism in Russia* (London, 1974); and Parkin, *Class Inequality*.

22. Zbigniew Brzezinski, *Ideology and Power in Soviet Politics*, 2d ed. (New York, 1967), esp. pp. 41–64; Robert C. Tucker, *The Marxian Revolutionary Idea* (Princeton, N.J., 1970), pp. 172–214; Seweryn Bialer, *Stalin's Successors: Leadership, Stability, and Change in the Soviet Union* (Cambridge, Eng., 1980), esp. pp. 45–46.

23. Brzezinski, *Ideology and Power*, pp. 49, 57–58.

24. See, for instance, Mao Zedong, "On Dialectics," U.S. Dept. of Commerce, Joint Publication Research Service, Feb. 20, 1974; "Is Yugoslavia a Socialist Country?" *Peking Review*, July 14, 1963, pp. 14–27; and "On Khrushchev's Phoney Communism," *Peking Review*, July 17, 1964, pp. 7–28. For a further bibliography of Mao on "bureaucratization, abuse of status, irrational rules, and routinization," see references under these headings in John B. Starr and Nancy A. Dyer, *Post-Liberation Works of Mao Zedong* (Berkeley, Calif., U.C. Center for Chinese Studies, 1976), p. 102.

25. Chalmers Johnson, "Comparing Communist Nations," in Johnson, ed., *Change in Communist Systems* (Stanford, Calif., 1970), pp. 1–33. See also Robert J. Lifton, *Revolutionary Immortality: Mao Tse-tung and the Chinese Cultural Revolution* (New York, 1968), and Richard D. Baum, "The New Revolution: Ideology Redivivus," *Problems of Communism*, 16 (May-June 1967): 1–21.

26. Johnson, "Comparing Communist Nations," p. 5.

27. Ibid., p. 7.   28. Ibid., p. 12.

29. Ibid., pp. 17, 25–26.   30. Ibid., p. 7.

31. For comprehensive bibliographies of the modernization literature as it relates to Communist systems, see Cohen and Shapiro, pp. xxi–xxxiii; and T. Anthony Jones, "Modernization Theory and Socialist Development," in Mark G. Field, ed., *Social Consequences of Modernization in Communist Societies* (Baltimore, Md., 1976), pp. 19–49.

32. John H. Kautsky, *Political Consequences of Modernization* (New York, 1972), p. 241.

33. R. C. Tucker, pp. 92–129; Kautsky, p. 249.

34. Theodore H. von Laue, *Why Lenin? Why Stalin?* (New York, 1971), p. 3.

35. Ibid., pp. 208–9.

36. Kautsky, p. 196.

37. Isaac Deutscher, *Russia: What Next?* (New York, 1953), pp. 123–24.

38. Ibid., pp. 124–25.

39. Zygmunt Bauman, "The Party in the Systems Management Phase," in Andrew C. Janos, ed., *Authoritarian Politics in Communist Europe* (Berkeley, Calif., U.C. Institute of International Studies Research Series, No. 28, 1976), pp. 81–109.

40. For a good survey of this literature, see Jones, pp. 19–49.

41. Ibid., pp. 44–47, nn. 36–51 and 69–80.

42. Marion J. Levy Jr., *Modernization and the Structure of Societies* (Princeton, N.J., 1966), p. 709.

43. Clark Kerr, J. T. Dunlop, F. H. Harbison, and C. A. Myers, *Industrialism and Industrial Man* (Cambridge, Mass., 1960), p. 42.

44. Ibid., pp. 42, 46.

45. Ibid., p. 46.

46. Reinhard Bendix, *Work and Authority in Industry*, 3d ed. (Berkeley, Calif., 1974), pp. xx–xlvi, 434–51. (First published 1956.)

47. Kenneth Jowitt, *Revolutionary Breakthroughs and National Development: The Case of Romania, 1945–66* (Berkeley, Calif., 1971), pp. 6–72. See also Jowitt, *The Leninist Response to National Dependency* (Berkeley, Calif., U.C. Institute of International Studies Research Series, No. 37, 1978).

48. In personal conversation with the author.

49. Kenneth Jowitt, "Soviet Neo-Traditionalism: The Political Concept of a Leninist Regime," *Soviet Studies*, 35 (July 1983): 275–97.

50. At least with respect to the Soviet Union. See Bialer, p. 163.

51. Immanuel Wallerstein, "The Rise and Future Demise of the

Capitalist World System," *Comparative Studies in Society and History*, 16 (1974): 387–415.

52. Striking, indeed gross, examples of this, including details of Western shopping trips, are to be found in the recollections of a recent high-ranking defector. See Arkady Shevchenko, *Breaking with Moscow* (New York, 1984).

53. Among numerous studies, see Konstantin Simis, *U.S.S.R.: The Corrupt Society* (New York, 1982).

54. See U.S. Dept. of State, *The Planetary Product* (Washington, D.C., Special Report No. 58, 1980), pp. 7–8.

55. Calculated by averaging the per capita GNP of six East European countries (Bulgaria, Czechoslovakia, Hungary, Poland, Romania, Yugoslavia) and comparing them with averages in seven advanced "Western" countries (U.S., Great Britain, France, Germany, Belgium, Sweden, Switzerland) in 1926–34 and in 1978. For the earlier date, see Colin Clark, *The Conditions of Economic Progress* (London, 1940); the 1978 figure is based on U.S. Dept. of State, *The Planetary Product*.

56. Immanuel Wallerstein, "Dependence in an Interdependent World: The Limited Possibilities of Transformation Within the Capitalist World Economy," *African Studies Review*, 18, No. 3 (Apr. 1974): 1–26.

57. Alexander Yanov, *The Russian New Right* (Berkeley, Calif., U.C. Institute of International Studies Research Series, No. 35, 1979).

Chapter 5

1. Karl Mannheim, *Man and Society in an Age of Reconstruction* (London, 1940), p. 43.

2. Ibid., p. 44.

3. Ibid., p. 53.

4. Jose Ortega y Gasset, *The Revolt of the Masses*, 25th anniversary ed. (New York, 1957), p. 56.

5. Ralf Dahrendorf, *Class and Class Conflict in Industrial Society* (Stanford, Calif., 1959), p. 57.

6. Daniel Bell, "The End of Ideology in the West," in *The End of Ideology: On the Exhaustion of Political Ideas in the Fifties* (New York, 1961), pp. 393–402, esp. 397. This ambiguous, yet often cited, essay speaks of "the search for a cause" and "almost pathetic anger" of the young generation. However, it also reiterates the "exhaustion of ideas" and the belief that the utopias of the future cannot rest on faith alone, but will require rationality and empiricism.

7. William Kornhauser, *The Politics of Mass Society*, 4th ed. (New York, 1965), pp. 47, 81.

8. Alex Inkeles and David H. Smith, *Becoming Modern: Individual Change in Six Developing Countries* (Cambridge, Mass., 1974), pp. 17–25.

9. Max Weber, *The Protestant Ethic and the Spirit of Capitalism*, Talcott Parsons, trans. (New York, 1958), p. 182.

10. Inkeles and Smith, pp. 5, 13.

11. Thomas S. Kuhn, *The Structure of Scientific Revolutions*, 1st ed. (Chicago, 1962), p. 18.

12. Morris Janowitz, *The Last Half-Century: Societal Change and Politics in America* (Chicago, 1978), p. 123.

13. Ibid., p. 19.

14. Ibid., p. 21.

15. Ibid., pp. 10–11.

16. Daniel Bell, *The Coming of Post-Industrial Society* (New York, 1973), p. 10.

17. Ibid., p. 13.

18. Ibid., p. 37.

19. Ibid., p. 112.

20. Ibid., p. 13.

21. Ibid.

22. Ibid., p. 363.

23. Ibid., p. 13.

24. Ibid.

25. Zbigniew K. Brzezinski, *Between Two Ages: America's Role in the Technetronic Revolution* (New York, 1970), p. xiv.

26. Ibid., p. 9.

27. Ibid., p. 54.

28. Ibid., pp. 203–4.

29. Ibid., pp. 225, 226, 111.

30. Louis Althusser, *Politics and History*, Ben Brewster, trans. (London, 1972); Nicos Poulantzas, *State, Power and Socialism*, Patrick Camiller, trans. (London, 1978); Joachim Hirsch, *Der Sicherheitsstaat: das Model Deutschland, seine Krise und die neuen sozialen Bewegungen* (Frankfurt, 1980); Wolf-Dieter Narr and Claus Offe, "Spätkapitalismus," in Narr and Offe, eds., *Wohlfahrtstaat und Massenloyalität* (Cologne, 1975), pp. 9–48; James O'Connor, "Die fiskalische Krise des Staates," in Narr and Offe, pp. 104–32. For a sympathetic discussion of this literature, see Martin Carnoy, *The State and Political Theory* (Princeton, N.J., 1984), pp. 65–152.

31. Poulantzas, p. 178.

32. Ibid., p. 217.

33. Ibid.

34. O'Connor, "Fiskalische Krise," p. 117. Also, in K. T. Fann and Donald C. Hodges, *Readings in U.S. Imperialism* (Boston, 1971), see William A. Williams, "The Vicious Circle of American Imperialism," pp. 117–26; Heather Dean, "Scarce Resources: The Dynamics of

American Imperialism," pp. 139–54; and Ernest Mandel, "Where Is America Going?" pp. 257–73.

35. Robert Gilpin, *U.S. Power and the Multinational Corporation* (New York, 1975), p. 70.

36. Carlo M. Cipolla, *Before the Industrial Revolution* (New York, 1976), p. 242.

37. Gilpin, p. 67.

38. Murray Bookchin, *Post-Scarcity Anarchism* (San Francisco, 1971).

39. Aaron Wildavsky, "The Revolt Against the Masses," in Wildavsky, *The Revolt Against the Masses and Other Essays on Politics and Public Policy* (New York, 1971), pp. 29–51.

40. Bell, *Post-Industrial Society*, p. 37.

41. Daniel Bell, *The Cultural Contradictions of Capitalism* (New York, 1976), p. 33.

42. Ibid., p. 10.

43. Ibid., p. 13.

44. Louis Althusser, *Lenin and Philosophy and Other Essays* (New York, 1971), p. 135. See also Carnoy, pp. 90–97.

45. Antonio Gramsci, *Selections from the Prison Notebooks*, Quintin Hoare and Geoffrey Smith, ed. and trans. (New York, 1971), esp. pp. 3, 45, 57–58.

46. Ibid., p. 66.

47. Translator's Introduction to Jürgen Habermas, *The Theory of Communicative Action*, vol. 1, Thomas McCarthy, trans. (Boston, 1984), pp. xvi, v.

48. Habermas, *Theorie des kommunikativen Handels*, vol. 2 (Frankfurt, 1981), p. 576. My translation; no English translation of vol. 2 was available at the time of writing.

49. Habermas, *Communicative Action*, p. xx.

50. Ibid., p. xxxii.

51. Pareto's major works in the original are *Cours d'économie politique*, 2 vols. (Paris, 1896–97) and *Trattato di sociologia generale*, 2 vols. (Florence, 1916); in English, *Mind and Society*, 4 vols., A. Bongiorno and A. Livingston, trans. (New York, 1935). Also Vilfredo Pareto, *The Rise and Fall of Elites* (Totowa, N.J., 1968). Mosca's works include *Elementi di scienza politica* (Turin, 1896); in English, *The Ruling Class*, H. D. Kahn, trans., with an introduction by A. Livingston (New York, 1939). For a bibliography and critical essay, see James H. Meisel, ed., *Pareto and Mosca* (Englewood Cliffs, N.J., 1965). Also T. B. Bottomore, *Elites and Society* (Baltimore, Md., 1964), esp. pp. 24–47.

52. Oswald Spengler's principal work, *The Decline of the West*, 2 vols. (New York, 1934), is available in a single-volume English edition

as *Today and Destiny: Excerpts from the Decline of the West,* Edwin F. Dakin, ed. (New York, 1940). References here are to this edited version.

53. Spengler, p. 71.

54. Ibid., p. 26.

55. Ibid.

56. See Talcott Parsons and Edward Shils, eds., *Toward a General Theory of Action,* 2d ed. (New York, 1962), p. 126. Also Clifford Geertz, "Ideology as a Cultural System," in David A. Apter, ed., *Ideology and Discontent* (Glencoe, Ill., 1965), pp. 47–72, esp. p. 62.

57. Habermas, *Communicative Action,* p. viii.

58. See Talcott Parsons, *Societies: Evolutionary and Comparative Perspectives* (Englewood Cliffs, N.J., 1966), pp. 5, 9, 20.

59. Kuhn, pp. 10–22.

60. Bell, *Cultural Contradictions,* p. 6.

61. Ibid.

62. David Hollinger, "T. S. Kuhn's Theory of Science and Its Implications for History," in Gary Cutting, ed., *Paradigms and Revolutions* (Notre Dame, Ind., 1980), pp. 199–200.

Conclusions

1. Siegfried Nagel, *The Theory of Social Structure* (London, 1957), esp. ch. 1.

2. Thorstein Veblen, *Imperial Germany and the Industrial Revolution,* 3d ed. (New York, 1954), p. 163.

3. Ibid., p. 132.

4. Clifford Geertz, "Thick Description: Toward an Interpretation of the Theory of Culture," in Geertz, *The Interpretation of Cultures* (New York, 1973), p. 29.

Index

DATE DUE

Library of Congress Cataloging-in-Publication Data

Janos, Andrew C.
  Politics and paradigms.

  Bibliography: p.
  Includes index.
    1.Political sociology—History.   2.Political
science—History.   3.Social change—History.
I.Title.
JA76.J34   1986   306'.2'09   86-3738
ISBN 0-8047-1332-4 (alk. paper)
ISBN 0-8047-1333-2 (pbk.)